Warman's
VIETNAM WAR
COLLECTIBLES

David Doyle

Identification and Price Guide

©2008 David Doyle

Published by

700 East State Street • Iola, WI 54990-0001
715-445-2214 • 888-457-2873
www.krausebooks.com

Our toll-free number to place an order or obtain
a free catalog is (800) 258-0929.

All rights reserved. No portion of this publication may be reproduced or transmitted in any form or by any means, electronic or mechanical, including photocopy, recording, or any information storage and retrieval system, without permission in writing from the publisher, except by a reviewer who may quote brief passages in a critical article or review to be printed in a magazine or newspaper, or electronically transmitted on radio, television, or the Internet.

Library of Congress Control Number: 2007942605
ISBN-13: 978-0-89689-604-8
ISBN-10: 0-89689-604-8

Designed by Donna Mummery
Edited by Mark Moran

Printed in China

Army.................8
Army Medical Department　8
Chaplain Corps　12
Chemical Corps　17
Corps of Engineers　22
Ordnance Corps　28
- Ammunition.................29
- Firearms.................31
- Accessories.................40
- Grenades.................48
- Knives & Bayonets.................50
- Mechanized.................53

Quartermaster Corps　68
- Boots.................69
- Headgear.................75
- Individual Equipment.................82
- Field Gear.................95
- Accoutrements.................106
- Uniforms.................119
- Subsistence and Survival Rations.................130

Signal Corps　142
Transportation Corps　154
Army Publications　182
Insignia　200
Personal Gear　203
Military Payment Certificates　212

Navy and Marines.................216
Air Force.................228
War Trophies.................240

Other titles in the Warman's® series

Identification and Price Guides

Antiques & Collectibles 2009 Price Guide
Carnival Glass
Children's Books
Civil War Collectibles
Civil War Weapons
Coca-Cola® Collectibles
Coins & Paper Money
Costume Jewelry Figurals
Depression Glass
Dolls: Antique to Modern
Duck Decoys
English & Continental Pottery & Porcelain
Fenton Glass
Fiesta
Flea Market Price Guide
Gas Station Collectibles
Hull Pottery
Jewelry
Little Golden Books®
Majolica
North American Indian Artifacts
Political Collectibles
Red Wing Pottery
Roseville Pottery
Sporting Collectibles
Sterling Silver Flatware
Weller Pottery
World War II Collectibles

Companions

Carnival Glass
Depression Glass
Fenton Glass
Fiesta
Hallmark Keepsake Ornaments
Hot Wheels®
McCoy Pottery
PEZ®
Roseville Pottery
U.S. Coins & Currency
World Coins & Currency

Dedication

Dedicated with humble thanks to the 2,700,000 U.S. servicemen and women who served in Vietnam, and their families, and those who remain unaccounted for today.

Acknowledgments

This book was a massive undertaking requiring a great deal of help from a number of dealers, collectors and museum curators. The diverse nature of equipment used in Vietnam, and the broad scope of this book, meant that no single source could hope to provide the necessary resources for this research.

Luther Hanson at the United States Army Quartermaster Museum was gracious enough to allow us to photograph many pieces of that fine collection for this book. Bill Paul with the Museum of Aviation at Robins Air Force Base near Macon, Ga., gave us access to various aviation artifacts for photography. Kip Lindberg with the Army Chemical Corps Museum at Fort Leonard Wood, Mo., was more than helpful in answering our questions and providing access. Marcia McManus, curator of the U.S. Army Chaplain Museum at Fort Jackson, S.C., allowed unfettered access to their equipment collection, and Jodie Wisemann at the Rock Island (Ill.) Arsenal Museum provided photographs of scarce and unusual weapons. Similar access was provided at the Army Signal Corps Museum at Ft. Gordon, Ga.

Private collectors pitched in as well – in fact, the bulk of the items shown here are from private collections. John Autry allowed access to his collection for photography, as he so often has done in the past. Advanced collectors David Bundy and Jeff Rowsam not only provided access to their collections, but allowed us to transport hundreds of items to the publisher's photo studio in order to get the shots "just right." David and Jeff also spent countless hours answering my seemingly unending questions by telephone and e-mail. Jon Shoop of www.tracksandthings.com was gracious in loaning many items for photography on several occasions, as well as helping with the descriptions and values of many of the weapons.

My father, Everette Doyle, also allowed me to haul items from his collection halfway across the nation for photographs. Dennis Mansker and Brian Wilder provided photos from their collections, as did Olivier Bizet of the http://grunts.free.fr Web site.

Bill Brewster, curator of collections at the Wisconsin Veterans Museum in Madison, provided the materials for the outstanding cover photograph, which was shot by Kris Kandler. The staff of the Veterans' Memorial Museum in Huntsville, Ala., opened their facility for us on a day normally closed, and removed many items from their display cases for us to photograph.

A special thanks is owed to Dan Brownell, who helped in editing this book. Dan, a veteran himself, provided valuable insight from the unique position as a professional editor and a veteran who was familiar with much of the gear herein. Mark Moran pushed, pulled, and prodded this project through its final stages, and his keen eye found many mistakes I'd missed, greatly improving the quality of the book. Donna Mummery not only did a great job with the layout of the book, but also found omissions and duplications that needed correction. My dear friend and fellow author, John Adams-Graf, provided frequent suggestions and recommendations, not only for content and style, but also for sources of information and photographs.

And a particular thank you to my fiancée, Denise, who often gave me words of encouragement as I periodically would become overwhelmed by the shear volume of material that had to be condensed to fit in this volume. Without such unqualified support and encouragement, I'd probably still be struggling with chapter 1!

WARMAN'S VIETNAM WAR COLLECTIBLES IDENTIFICATION AND PRICE GUIDE

Introduction

The Vietnam War is a unique part of the American experience. Previous generations of soldiers had gone to war with the almost unanimous support of the American people – not only morally, but in a sense, physically as well. The earlier wars had brought about shortages of goods at home, and oftentimes rationing was needed on certain commodities. Not so with Vietnam. There were no campaigns here to eat less meat so our soldiers abroad could have more, no scrap drives asking each American to do their part to defeat the distant enemy.

Introduction

With the Vietnam War, the American people left the soldier to fight on his own – without the camaraderie with civilians that had been felt in WWI, WWII and Korea. Worse, politicians in Washington DIDN'T leave the soldier's to fight on the own. Too many politicians and bureaucrats inserted themselves in the fighting in a broad range of areas, from weapons selection to absurd rules of engagement.

Television thrust the war into Middle America's living room night after night, adding fuel to the fires of the political forces who wanted U.S. troops withdrawn. Protesters in the streets derided U.S. servicemen as "baby killers" and "war mongers" – protests that, had they occurred only two decades earlier, would likely have been met by lynch mobs.

Service in America's armed forces – the pride of the nation in 1945 – was by some media accounts something to be ashamed of during the Vietnam War. It is not surprising then that many returning veterans discarded their uniforms and gear, or stowed them away in footlockers in dusty attics or damp basements.

Over time though, America has begun to realize that the men and women who served in Vietnam were just as honorable, dedicated and patriotic as their father's who'd fought in WWII. Perhaps because the troops in Vietnam fought under such hardship and derision, children and grandchildren are asking about the Vietnam experience.

Living-history events and reenactments, long centered on the Civil War or WWII, are now expanding and including Vietnam, as well. Though no single volume could possibly list all the types of equipment used or encountered by troops in Vietnam, in this book I've shown those most frequently found tucked into old duffel bags, or shown in snapshots, or mentioned in the telling of old war stories.

The values given are for new or excellent-condition unissued items in most instances. Items known to have been used in Vietnam, with documented provenance, command premium prices, but that provenance is essential. Many a larcenous individual has merely picked up a piece of surplus equipment, drawn Vietnam-style markings on it, and declared it to have been from a Veteran's estate. Similarly, many Internet sellers offer gear claiming it to be Vietnam-era issue, yet the contract dates clearly prove otherwise. It is for this reason that throughout this book are shown close-ups of the contract dates, labels and Federal Stock Number, to help differentiate between the "same as Vietnam-issue" and the authentic item.

The United States was involved in Vietnam longer than any other war. President Eisenhower sent the first U.S. military advisors to Vietnam on Feb. 12, 1955. Official U.S. military involvement in Vietnam ended on March 29, 1973, though the last U.S. troop casualty was April 29, 1975, during the evacuation of the U.S. embassy in Saigon.

However, for 1,992 unaccounted-for men and women, and their families, the war is not yet over.

ARMY

Care for the wounded in Vietnam benefited tremendously from the helicopter. Wounded men could be whisked from the battlefield to fully-equipped medical facilities in a matter of minutes, but the first line of defense was the soldier's own first-aid kit. National Archives photo.

Army Medical Department

Medical care for U.S. personnel was of critical importance virtually from the outset of America's involvement in Vietnam. In December 1961 a field hospital with 100-bed capacity, four attached medical detachments and one helicopter ambulance detachment were authorized for deployment in Vietnam. This field hospital became operational in April of 1961. At that time this branch of the Army was known as the Army Medical Service, but on June 4, 1968, the name reverted to Army Medical Department, as it had been known prior to the Army Organization Act of 1950.

ARMY: MEDICAL DEPARTMENT

This bag was devised as a means to keep a patient's effects dry and handy. However, because they were waterproof, they became popular with troops in the field who used them as ditty bags..$5-15

The triangular bandage shown at right was also popular as a bandana or sweat rag. It was often used as a sweat rag. These were widely carried by soldiers in the field, as well as being a component of most first-aid kits.......... $5-10

A 101st Airborne trooper comforts a wounded comrade. A field dressing has been applied to the wounded GI's head. Rapid evacuation of the wounded to relatively advanced medical facilities lessened the percentage of troops killed in action in Vietnam compared to prior conflicts, with a slight increase in the number of amputations. Photo courtesy of Don F. Pratt Museum, Ft. Campbell, Ky.

This wounded trooper awaiting evacuation from Landing Zone Bronco in Cambodia in June 1970 has been bandaged with a white Field Dressing. Olive drab field dressings were also developed. National Archives photo.

Early on, the battle dressing was white, with red coding to indicate the side to be placed toward the wound. The dressing was carried in a canvas pouch – the same type pouch as used for the Lensatic compass.........$10-20

The Jungle First Aid Kit pouch was replaced by this nylon Medical Instrument and Supply Set Case No. 8 containing the Individual First Aid Kit beginning in 1969. The soft nylon outer shell was closed by two metal wsnaps, and a pair of metal slides was provided to secure the kit to the utility belt..............................$25-35

ARMY: MEDICAL DEPARTMENT

Litters, such as this one being used at Can Tho Army Airfield Vietnam in June 1970, were widely used in the preliminary evacuation of wounded. National Archive photo.

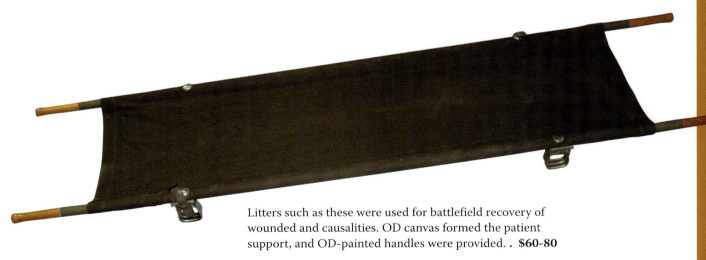

Litters such as these were used for battlefield recovery of wounded and causalities. OD canvas formed the patient support, and OD-painted handles were provided. . **$60-80**

The Army issued only a moderate amount of equipment to chaplains, so they often relied on personal supplies to further their ministry to the troops. Here is a typical expedient altar prepared using a Protestant Chaplain's kit in a 81mm mortar pit in Cambodia. National Archives Photo.

Chaplain Corps

Men dealing with the horrors of combat, the stress of separation from their loved ones, and a host of other tribulations turn to the men of the Chaplain Corps for solace. Troops in Vietnam were no exception, and on Feb. 26, 1962, Chaplain John A. Lindvall arrived in Vietnam, becoming the first of over 300 Army chaplains to arrive in country. Two of these men were awarded the Medal of Honor, and 13 chaplains and 8 chaplain assistants died in Vietnam.

As the chaplains were required to be ordained ministers of their faith, many brought with them the "gear" they needed. Still others fashioned altarware in country, although the Army ultimately issued lightweight chaplain's kits for Jewish, Protestant and Catholic faiths. Relatively few of these kits appear on the surplus markets.

ARMY: Chaplain Corps

REGIMENTAL FLAG

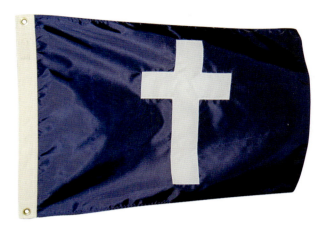

The Chaplain Corps flag for the Christian faith consists of a Latin cross on a dark blue background $25-50

The Chaplain Corps flag for the Jewish faith consists of a Of the tablets with the Star of David on a dark blue background $25-50

DISTINCTIVE INSIGNIA
During the Vietnam War, two types of distinctive insignia were authorized for wear with the chaplain's uniform. Christian distinctive insignia consisted of a Latin Cross.
.... $10-20
Jewish chaplains wore distinctive insignia comprised of tablets with the Star of David. $20-30

CHAPLAIN KIT
Broadly speaking, three types of Chaplain's kits were used in Vietnam, one each for Catholic, Jewish and Protestant. The content of the kit naturally varied as appropriate with the faith.

EARLY CATHOLIC CHAPLAIN KIT
Packaged in a heavy metal box, the Catholic Chaplain kit is most readily identified by a crucifix for the altar, rather than the cross found in Protestant kits. This type of kit, which weighed about 24 pounds, was too heavy to be easily portable, and efforts were made to develop a lighter version.
.... $1,800-2,000

On the beach at Cam Rahn Bay in June 1967, a chaplain's assistant prepares for Jewish religious services using the early-type chaplain's kit. A Jewish chaplain's flag has been stretched across the windshield of the M151. National Archives photo.

EARLY JEWISH CHAPLAIN KIT
Similar in construction to the Catholic kit listed above, the lid of the case included a partus (Ark hangings) behind which was stored a Torah with cover. The kit also included a Torah pointer, a Kiddush cup, two candlesticks and a plastic bottle. **$2,400-2,600**

ARMY: Chaplain Corps

LATE PROTESTANT CHAPLAIN KIT
In order to make the chaplain's kit more mobile in the field, a lightweight kit was developed, which used a nylon case rather than the metal case used previously. These were provided in Catholic, Jewish and Protestant versions, the Protestant version (with cross rather than crucifix) is shown here. **$1,000-1,200**

Chaplain (Maj) Daniel Barnabas holds Mass using the late lightweight Chaplain's kit in June 1970. The service is being conducted at Fire Base Exodus in Vietnam. National Archives photo.

Musical Equipment

For many faiths, music is important part of the worship service. Accordingly, Chaplains often went to great effort to provide musical accompaniment for the worship service.

Tipping the scales at almost 65 pounds, the field organ was the used in the early stages of the Vietnam War. A descendant of the WWII field organ, the Vietnam-era organs differed by being natural wood finish rather than olive drab, and carrying LoDuca Bros. nameplates rather than Estey. Their wooden construction was not well suited to the tropics. In addition, their heavy weight and early war usage also contribute to only two surviving examples known to have been used in country.

. . . .**Too rarely traded to establish accurate pricing.**

TAPE RECORDER/PLAYER
The heavy, bulky field organ was succeeded by this lightweight transistor reel-to-reel tape unit. Chaplains were provided with one of these units and a library of recordings to use in the field. $50-100

ARMY: CHEMICAL CORPS

Chemical Corps

Tear gas, smoke grenades and a few other munitions used by U.S. troops in Vietnam were within the purview of the Chemical Corps. Prior to the U.S. entry in Vietnam (1952, specifically) the Army's mortars were "Chemical Mortars" – and were also a Chemical Corps responsibility. This was due to their use in laying smoke screens. Because many still think of mortars in this traditional manner, they are also included in this chapter, though by the Vietnam era, they were Ordnance Corps responsibility.

The M17 gas mask was the standard-issue gas mask during the Vietnam War. Though it offered no protection from ammonia, smoke or radiation, the mask protected against most other inhalation hazards. The only troops in Vietnam who routinely wore the gas mask were those involved in riot control, or the famed "tunnel rats," who used tear gas to flush Viet Cong from their maze of tunnels and passages.

The canvas bag for the gas mask was an entirely different matter, and it was extremely popular with troops who used the bag to transport assorted personal effects. $20-50

Warman's Vietnam War Collectibles Identification and Price Guide

Without intervention, the eyepieces of gas masks fog when worn, reducing visibility for the wearer. The army developed this Antifogging Kit, M1, which consisted of a special cloth packed in a screw-top plastic container roughly the size of a film canister. After each wearing the soldier was to moisten the mask lens with his fingertips, then rub with this cloth before returning the mask to storage. **$1-3**

During the early stages of the war in Vietnam, GIs were issued WWII-surplus "anti-dim cloth." Functionally the same as the later M1 Antifogging Kit, this version was packed in a small tin tube with removable top. **$3-5**

ARMY: CHEMICAL CORPS

Red and yellow smoke grenades have been popped to signal these "C" Troop, 3rd Squadron, 4th Cavalry, 11th Armored Cavalry M113 armored personnel carriers crossing the border back into Vietnam from Cambodia in June 1970. National Archives photo.

The M18 smoke grenade generated a cloud of colored smoke lasting 50 to 90 seconds. The top of the canister was painted in a color indicative of the smoke color generated. The example here would generate green smoke, but red, yellow and violet smoke grenades were also produced. The M18 weighed 19 ounces and used a M201A1 fuse. **$60-80**

WARMAN'S VIETNAM WAR COLLECTIBLES IDENTIFICATION AND PRICE GUIDE

Red smoke has been popped to guide a helicopter in for a landing at Fire Base Exodus in June 1970. The smoke grenades delivered copious amounts of smoke, but for less than two minutes. National Archives photo.

This M18 produces red smoke. Different colors of smoke were used for signaling, particularly for helicopter evacuation. Viet Cong guerillas captured so much allied radio gear, and so many smoke grenades, great care had to be used to avoid being drawn into an ambush. Ultimately, the ground troops would not tell the helicopter pilots what color of smoke they were going to discharge (else the VC would "pop" the same color). Rather, the helicopter crews would call out the color they saw, and the ground forces would verify................................$60-80

ARMY: CHEMICAL CORPS

The 81mm mortar used by the U.S. forces in Vietnam, the M29, had been developed in the 1950s to replace the WWII-era M1 81mm mortar. The mortar assembly weighed about 100 pounds, and could be broken down for transport, with one man carrying the base plate, another the tube, and another the bipod. Typical usage was by mortar platoon within an infantry battalion. The M29 was a smooth bore, muzzle-loaded, high-angle, indirect fire weapon with a minimum range of 76 yards and a maximum of 3,990 yards.
. . . . $1,000-2,000

Several types of rounds could be fired by the 81mm mortar, including light and heavy high explosive, white phosphorus and illumination. Of course, inert training rounds were produced as well. $75-100

The 4.2-inch (107mm) chemical mortar was a fearsome weapon, firing a 24- to 26-pound shell 6,500 yards. It was generally considered regimental artillery, and because of its shear size and weight (626 pounds) was not considered man-portable, and in fact was often mounted in a variation of the M113 armored personnel carrier known as the M106. Unlike the 81mm mortar, the tube of the 4.2-inch mortar was rifled. $1,600-2,500

"Rome Plows" — the name of the blade itself having come to be used to refer to the bulldozers equipped with these special tree-clearing blades — were used to push back wide swathes of foliage along highways, denying shelter to VC ambush teams. The dozer operators were prime sniper targets. These men of the 984th Land Clearing Company, 11th Cavalry, work with the protection of M113 APCs in December 1969. National Archives photo.

Corps of Engineers

Throughout the war in Vietnam, America tried to win the hearts, and support, of the native peoples. A large part of this campaign was extensive public works projects – roads, bridges, buildings, etc. While much of this work was done by private contractors, notably Pacific Architects and Engineers, the nearer the work got to areas involved in fighting, the more likely the work was to be carried out by the Army Engineers.

The array of equipment used by these men is mind boggling – ranging from hammers to road graders to entire concrete plants. Engineer items alone could fill a volume many times the size of the one in your hands now. While there are those enthusiasts who collect such equipment (including this author), most of the gear falls outside the interests of mainstream collectors. Hence, for this chapter, the discussion will be confined to those items likely to be used in "living history" displays.

ARMY: Corps of Engineers

Development of mine-detection equipment is a Corps of Engineers responsibility. The AN/PSS-11 mine detector was one of the most commonly used units in Vietnam. Several different firms produced these mine detectors, with each manufacturer assigning their own model number. Among these were Polan P153, P158, P190; Oregon MD-M; VP Company VP200; and Fourdee 4D5000.
................................$50-100

It was the day after Christmas 1969 when this photo was snapped of 11th Cavalry troopers sweeping a road for mines in Vietnam. This was an unenvied job indeed. National Archives photo.

This is a hand-held demolition engineer's 10 Cap Blasting Machine. The machine is connected to the charge by two wires connected to the threaded terminals. The removable handle is twisted to generate a small electrical current sufficient to fire up to 10 blasting caps in series. There is also a larger model, the 50 Cap Blasting Machine with a T-handle plunger. $200-300

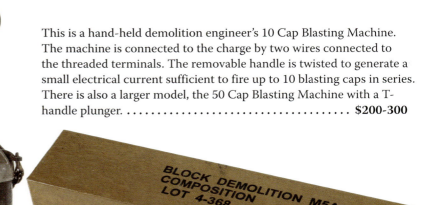

The M5A1 Composition C-4 demolition block contains C-4 explosive, which is 91% RDX and has no odor. The block is formed of 2 1/2 pounds of C-4 in a plastic container with a threaded blasting cap recess at each end. Possession of actual C-4 is strictly regulated, but dummy training blocks as shown here are popular collector's items. $10-20

Engineers also used blocks of trinitrotoluene, or TNT. These were issued in 1/4-, 1/2- and 1-pound blocks, with metal ends that were threaded for blasting caps. Once again, possession of the real thing is regulated, but the dummy training aids are found in many collections. $8-15

Members of the Explosive Ordnance Disposal Team (EOD), 27th Battalion, 18th Brigade, 45th Engineer Group, 101st Airborne Division are attaching a blasting cap to a length of detonation cord in this February 1971 photo. This was taken at the old Marine base at Khe Sanh, in an effort to clear the perimeter. National Archives photo.

ARMY: CORPS OF ENGINEERS

Detonation cord, also known as "det cord" or primer cord, is a thin, flexible tube with an explosive core. It was used as a high-speed fuse that explodes, rather than burns, and was suitable for triggering high explosives. The det cord itself is initiated with a blasting cap.

This is the plastic storage box that holds up to 10 M6 electric blasting caps used by engineers to fire demolition charges. The caps are dangerous and are held in 10 separate vertical openings in the box. They were used with the hand-held 10-cap blasting machine. **$15-30**

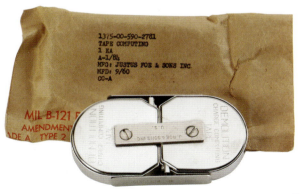

The Demolition Charge Computing Tape was essentially a pocket-sized analog computer used to calculate the size charge needed to demolish structures made of various materials and of various sizes. One side of the case reads "Demolition Charge Computing Tape," the other side of the case is embossed "Rods, bars, chain, cable; Do not use for rectangles if ratio exceeds 2 to 1; Calibrated for TNT."
.... **$30-40**

This demolition haversack is part of the U.S. Army combat engineer demolition kit (the "satchel charge" of Hollywood fame). The bag is a purpose-built, heavy water-repellant canvas material intended to contain eight M5A1 blocks of C-4 explosive along with two non-electric primers and detonation cord. The kit weighed 22 pounds complete, which explains the heavy web shoulder strap for transport. The bag measures 4 inches by 8 inches by 11 inches tall. Some manuals refer to the bag as an M-85 carrying case. The bag with contents is designated as Charge Assembly, Demolition M-37. There are extra straps that tie around the bag to hold the contents secured in place within the bag. Combat Engineer slang for any bag carrying explosives is called a "lightening bag," for obvious reasons............ **$15-35**

Company C, 27th Engineer Battalion, 45th Engineer Group, supervises members of Company C, 1st ARVN Engineer Battalion, 1st ARVN Division, who are building a bridge near Hue in August 1969. Engineers used a bewildering array of equipment, with this Cat D7E bulldozer one of the middle-sized items. National Archives photo.

ARMY: Corps of Engineers

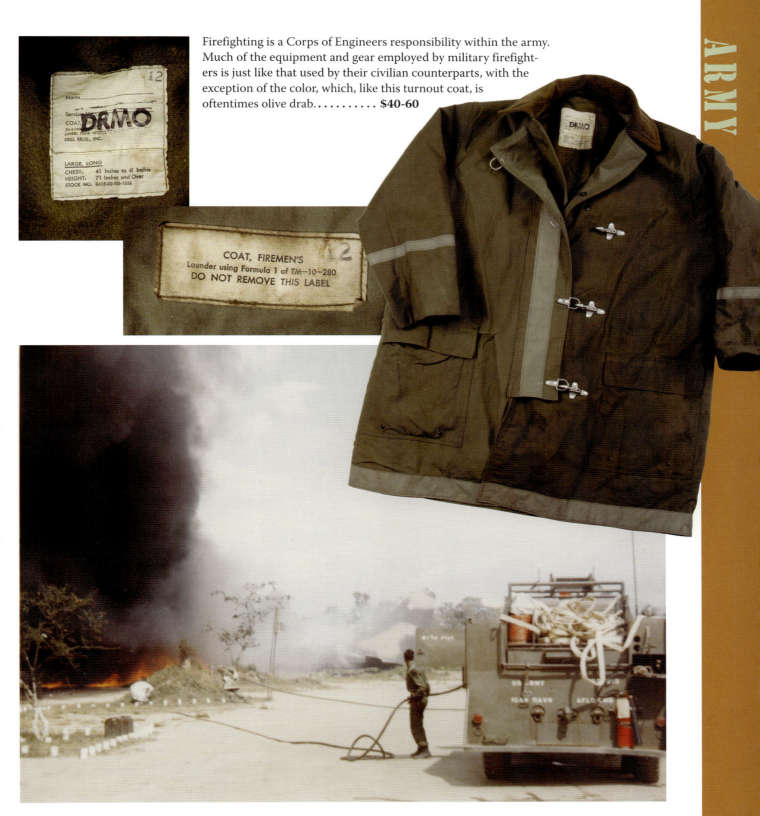

Firefighting is a Corps of Engineers responsibility within the army. Much of the equipment and gear employed by military firefighters is just like that used by their civilian counterparts, with the exception of the color, which, like this turnout coat, is oftentimes olive drab. **$40-60**

Army firefighters with 1st Cavalry struggle to extinguish a blazing C-130 that crashed after take off from An Khe in March 1967. National Archives photo.

Ordnance Corps

For the most part, the items that separate a soldier from a civilian are the responsibility of the Ordnance Corps. Guns – ranging from artillery to pistols, knives, grenades and the like – are all supplied through the Ordnance Corps. For ease of locating, this broad array of items has been divided into sub groupings by type. All the items here are available on the collector market, but some are much more difficult and expensive to obtain than others.

Many of these items are highly regulated, with stiff penalties for failure to comply with national and local laws. This adds to the "mystique" of many ordnance items, notably machine guns, artillery pieces and tanks. Compliance with some of these laws is costly, and this further drives up pricing.

The pricing found in the firearms portion of this book is different than that found in the remainder of the book. For the most part, collectors shun reproductions or fakes; however, an exception seems to exist in this regard when it comes to weapons. A firearm is a key part of many Vietnam displays, exhibits and mannequin dressing. In many areas, regulation has made this difficult, particularly if items are displayed publicly, especially at schools. Hence, a legitimate market has developed for demilitarized or dummy weapons, as well as automatic weapon replicas capable of firing as semi-automatics. Hence, pricing is given for live, fully automatic, legally transferable weapons, semi-automatic variants, and demilitarized or dummy weapons.

Similarly, the grenades and rockets shown here are either demilitarized or expended. This is NOT the same thing as an inert or dummy grenade—the latter being much more common and much less valuable or desirable than the examples here.

Armored fighting vehicles and self-propelled weapons are also listed in this chapter. Collecting this equipment is a hobby unto itself; however, many vehicle collectors completely outfit their vehicles with period gear and wear authentic clothing while operating them. Private ownership of these vehicles is legal in the United States, although some localities have imposed restrictions. Many of the armored vehicles used in the Vietnam War are still being used by U.S. soldiers today, and hence are not readily available on the market. Also, the Department of Defense has severely curtailed the sales of such vehicles domestically, while the State Department is not currently allowing any such vehicles to be repatriated. Cannon ownership, whether mounted on a vehicle or towed, is also legal. However, if the cannon is capable of firing, its breech must be registered with the Bureau of Alcohol, Tobacco and Firearms (BATF) as a destructive device. The values indicated for these items assume a non-firing gun. Be aware that the army considers most tanks, armored vehicles and cannons on display at VFW's, American Legions and city parks to still be federal property. Do not consider buying or trading for such an item without an irrefutable chain of title, including a release from the federal government.

ARMY: ORDNANCE CORPS

AMMUNITION:

U.S. Forces in Vietnam used a wide variety of ammunition. Ammunition collecting is a special niche, and while collectors specialize in collecting spent or inert rounds for artillery and the like, small-arms ammunition is more commonly collected.

The 7.62mm Ball M80 ammunition was the standard round for the M14 rifle carried by U.S. troops when first deployed to Vietnam. Some of the ammunition was shipped in these 20-round cardboard boxes. The M60 machine gun also fired this round.
.............................$20-30

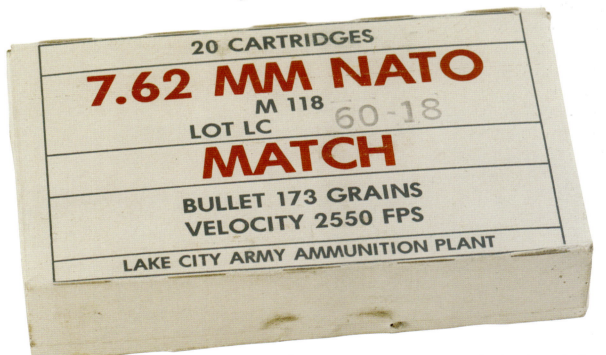

The M118 7.62mm ammunition was developed specifically for high-accuracy weapons. This included the M21, M24 and M40A1 sniper rifles, as well as M14s used in competitive shooting. Obviously, this ammo was produced in much smaller quantities than the standard M80 ball ammunition.
.... $40-50

The 105mm howitzer has been the primary artillery support for U.S. troops since World War II. The M101A1 was the army's standard 105 at the beginning of the Vietnam War. The weapon was reliable and easy to use. The waist-high breech made loading easy, but the 4,980-pound weight hindered mobility, particularly for airborne units. A well-trained crew could fire 10 rounds per minute with the M101A1, but a three-round per minute sustained rate was more practical. . . . .**Demilitarized $2,000; Transferable, live-firing $25,000**

ARMY: ORDNANCE CORPS

FIREARMS

Aircrews in Vietnam, including those of Army helicopters and recon aircraft, were issued the .38 Smith and Wesson. This particular example is shown with a locally made holster. $200-500

As its name would suggest, the basic form of this pistol was adopted in 1911. The M1911A1 used in Vietnam (and Korea and WWII) dates from 1924. This semi-automatic pistol was designed by John Browning. The M1911A1s used in Vietnam had actually been produced during WWII or before. Hence, these are popular with collectors of many eras, and their reliability and stopping power keep these guns in demand with casual shooters, as well. There are many variations of this gun, and the collecting of the M1911A1 is a hobby unto itself. The value here is for the most common Colt-made weapons. $800-1,200

Armed with the iconic M16A1, members of Troop B, 1st Squadron, 9th Cavalry, 1st Cavalry Division, move through the An Lao Valley in July 1967. The M16 was a radical departure from previous weapons designs, but many soldiers in Vietnam did not think it was an improvement. National Archives photo.

Many scholars consider the M14 to be the best rifle fielded by the U.S. during the Vietnam War. Indeed, there are many that consider the M14 the finest battle rifle *ever* carried by U.S. servicemen. A derivative of the earlier M1 Garand, the M14 was produced from July 1959 through June 1964, with production totaling 1,380,358 rifles. It was the Army's standard rifle until the M16 was introduced. At that time it was gradually withdrawn from service, with frontline troops turning their weapons in first, followed by those in rear areas and support operations.

The automatic M14 fired 7.62mm ball ammunition, and was favored for its range, accuracy and stopping power. The gun was fed from a detachable 20-round box magazine, and with a full magazine and cleaning kit weighed 11.22 pounds. This weight was considered a disadvantage, and played a large role in the M14 being replaced.

Transferable fully automatic $15,000-22,000
Semi-automatic. $1,000-1,200
Demilitarized. $350-1,000

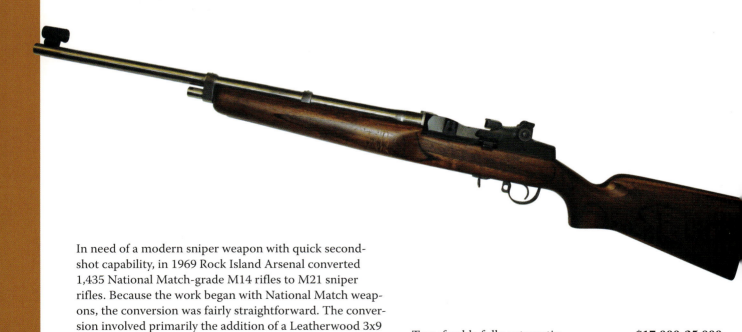

In need of a modern sniper weapon with quick second-shot capability, in 1969 Rock Island Arsenal converted 1,435 National Match-grade M14 rifles to M21 sniper rifles. Because the work began with National Match weapons, the conversion was fairly straightforward. The conversion involved primarily the addition of a Leatherwood 3x9 adjusting range telescopic sight. The resulting weapon was notably accurate, and remains in use with U.S. armed forces today. When used with National Match ammunition, the M21 has a range of 750 yards.

Transferable fully automatic $17,000-25,000
Semi-automatic. $2,500-2,000
Demilitarized. $350-1,000

ARMY: ORDNANCE CORPS

The M1 Thompson submachine gun was adopted for U.S. service in 1942, replacing the previous, and similar looking, M1928A1 Thompson. Even before WWII was over the M1 had been replaced by the simpler M1A1 Thompson. Both of these were officially obsolete by the time large number of U.S. troops entered Vietnam. However, the Hollywood image of these guns made them popular with troops, who often were able to obtain the Thompson from ARVN officers, whose army had been supplied the weapons by the United States. The same Hollywood mystique captivates many collectors today.

Transferable fully automatic $15,000-20,000
Semi-automatic. $1,000-1,200
Demilitarized. $350-1,000

Although officially obsolete during the U.S. involvement in Vietnam, several of the famed M1A1 Thompson submachine guns were in the war-torn country, having been supplied to the ARVN. The U.S. had also supplied numbers of these weapons to China during and following WWII, and reportedly some of these guns came to be used by the Viet Cong. In any event, a number of these submachine guns found their way into the hands of U.S. troops deployed to Vietnam. With classic looks, noted reliability, and easy access to ammunition (the Thompson fired the same ammunition as the M1911A1 pistol) many soldiers added the "Tommy gun" to their personal arsenal.

Transferable fully automatic $15,000-20,000
Semi-automatic. $1,000-1,200
Demilitarized. $350-1,000

The M3A1 .45-caliber submachine gun, popularly known as the "grease gun," was developed during WWII as a low-cost, easily produced replacement for the Thompson submachine gun. During WWII, the Guide Lamp Division of General Motors, the originator of the design, produced the gun, and during the Korean War, Ithaca manufactured additional copies.

By the time the United States entered Vietnam, the Army no longer used the "grease gun," but the weapon continued to be used by Marine armored crewmen.

Transferable fully automatic $18,000-20,000
Semi-automatic $1,000-1,200
Demilitarized $300-500

The M16 has become the symbol of the U.S. GI in Vietnam. The design of the weapon originated with Eugene Stoner, and was licensed to Colt for production. Initial procurement was by the Air Force, whose security troops used the weapon. After considerable testing in 1965, the M16 was type classified Standard A and became the issue rifle of soldiers in Vietnam. Once fielded, the weapons were found to be terribly susceptible to jamming and hence were unpopular with troops—particularly the Marines. The M16 fired a .223 (5.56mm) cartridge, and was rifled with 1-in-12 twist. While the test articles had a 1-in-14 twist that produced a bullet tumble that was devastating to targets, the tighter rifling, required to get the desired accuracy, negated the tumble, and hence were much less injurious to enemy personnel.

Live, transferable $11,000-20,000
Demilitarized $400-700

ARMY: ORDNANCE CORPS

In 1967 an improved model was introduced, the M16A1. This weapon had been redesigned in an effort to eliminate the jamming problems common in the earlier model. The A1 was classified as Standard A in 1967. Like the M16, the M16A1 was capable of semi-automatic and automatic fire, with a practical rate of 60 rounds per minute. The weapon had an effective range of 300 meters.

Live, transferable......................$14,000-16,000
Demilitarized.............................. $400-700

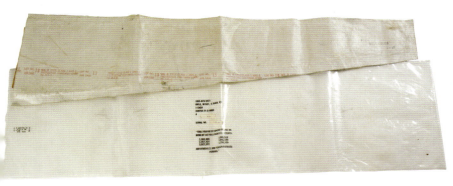

New M16s were shipped in two layers of packaging to preserve and protect the weapon. Today, this packaging is far more difficult to find than the weapon itself................ $100

SP4 Ronald Krug loads his M79 grenade launcher just outside Saigon in December 1968. The M79 could fire a variety of munitions, but its most frequent use in Vietnam was for firing tear-gas rounds, like the one being loaded here. National Archives photo.

Warman's Vietnam War Collectibles Identification and Price Guide

Frequently referred to as "Thumper" or "Blooper", the M79 was first issued in 1961. Rather resembling a large, short, shotgun, the M79 was a single-shot, break-barrel weapon firing a 40mm grenade. Its intended use was for ranges between hand-thrown grenades and mortars. Two M79-armed grenadiers served in each rifle company. These men, in addition to being armed with the M79, also carried M1911A1 pistols. $6,000-8,000

The M203 grenade launcher was designed to be attached to the M16A1 rifle, to negate the need for the separate M79 grenade launcher. This was a semi-permanent attachment performed by armorers. The 12-inch long rifled grenade launcher fired 40mm ammunition, which came in a variety of forms, including smoke, high explosive, illuminating, high-explosive dual purpose, and a variety of others.

The weapon had a range of about 400 yards, but was not notable for its accuracy. The M203 is classified as a "Destructive Device" by the National Firearms Act, and is appropriately regulated.

M203 alone $2,000-5,000

The XM177E2, often known as the Colt Commando, was derived from the XM177E1, itself based on the XM177, which was a variation of the M16. The XM177E2, of which only 510 were produced in 1967, were supplied to MACV-SOG. Colt assigned the weapon their model number 629. Many more – 2,815 specifically – of the earlier XM177E1 had been produced.

The XM177E2 was essentially a shortened M16 with an 11.5-inch barrel and a telescoping stock. The gun was issued to a limited number of elite units, but was plagued with range, accuracy and fouling problems. $14,000-20,000

Demilitarized. $500-1,000

ARMY: ORDNANCE CORPS

Hard-rubber replica M16 rifles were made for training purposes. Known as "Rubber Duckies," these were familiar to all GI's who went through basic training in the later part of the Vietnam War. $200-225

The M1919A4 .30-caliber machine gun had served GIs through WWII and Korea, but by the time U.S. troops arrived in Vietnam in significant numbers, it had been rendered obsolete. However, significant numbers had been supplied as military assistance to ARVN, and limited numbers remained in the U.S. inventory. Because of its long service history with the U.S. military, many soldiers in Vietnam were familiar with the M1919A4, and employed it whether or not authorized. Fed by 250-round belts, the weapon had a 400-500 round per minute cyclic rate, and weighed 31 pounds. The bulk of the roughly 450,000 M1919A4s purchased by the military were made by the Saginaw Steering Gear Div. of General Motors, although Rock Island Arsenal and Buffalo Arms Co. each produced just over 30,000 weapons.

Transferable full-auto $13,000-15,000
Semi-auto $1,000-1,100
Dummy $300-500

The M60 was the primary squad weapon in the jungles of Vietnam. With a maximum rate of fire of 550 rounds per minute, the gun had a voracious appetite for ammunition, and the gunner and his assistant typically carried all they could. National Archives photo.

The German MG42 machine gun of WWII is arguably one of the best-engineered weapons of that war. Not surprisingly, captured examples of these guns were carefully studied during the war, and for some time afterward. Drawing from these studies, the M60 general-purpose machine gun was developed, and production began in 1957. Notable characteristics drawn from the MG42 are the quick-change barrel and the feed mechanism.

The 7.62mm M60 was used as a door-mount weapon on helicopters, as well as a mounted weapon on various tactical vehicles, but its primary use was as a squad weapon. For this use, the weapon was equipped with a bipod. Infantrymen in Vietnam complained about the weapon's 23-pound weight and tendency to jam, particularly when exposed to dust. The gun was supplied with an asbestos glove to be used when changing barrels hot from sustained fire.

Transferable full-auto . . . . $30,000-$35,000
Semi-auto $7.500-8,500
Dummy $1,000-5,000

The Browning .50-caliber machine gun was the Army's primary heavy machine gun in Vietnam, as it had been in WWII and Korea, and continues to be to this day. The .50-caliber design dates to 1921. Considered by many to be John Browning's finest design, was originally water cooled. In 1932, an air-cooled version for ground use was developed. This version had a barrel with thicker walls to withstand heat. This resulted in the barrel being denoted heavy, and the weapon we know today as the .50-caliber machine gun is properly the M2 HB (Heavy Barrel) machine gun. Though widely used on various vehicle mountings, the M2 was designed as an infantry weapon. In this use, the 84-pound machine gun was mounted on a M2 tripod, which weighed a further 44 pounds.

The gun has a cyclic rate of fire of 450-550 rounds per minute, but rates of less than 40 rounds per minute are typical in use. The maximum range of the weapon is 4.5 miles, although its effective range is about 1.2 miles.

Transferable full-auto $23,000-35,000
Semi-auto $8,500-10,000
Dummy $1,000-5,000

ARMY: ORDNANCE CORPS

The M72 Light Antitank Weapon (LAW) was originally developed as an infantry weapon to combat the hordes of Soviet tanks that threatened Europe during the Cold War. It was classified as Standard in March 1961. Because the Communists made only limited use of armored vehicles in Vietnam, the LAW was most frequently used for bunker busting. The lightweight (about 5 pounds) disposable weapon was not rifled. With the end covers shut, the weapon was watertight. To fire the weapon, the end covers were opened and an inner tube slid out. This action cocked the launcher. The 1-kilo rocket, which had a 66mm high-explosive antitank warhead, was fired by pulling a trigger, and the launcher discarded. It had an effective range of 300m. While the LAW launcher is harmless and unregulated, the rocket itself is a BATF "destructive device" and is regulated accordingly. . . . . **$200-225 tube only**

M72A1
The first M72 LAWs used in Vietnam were notable for their failure to fire. Immediately, efforts were made to counter this, and the M72A1 shown here was fielded in response to this. Even this was not sufficient, and a third variant, the M72A2, was also developed and used in Vietnam, further enhancing reliability. . . . . **$200-225 tube only**

Accessories

These buff-colored pasters were used to repair targets on training ranges both in the U.S. and in Vietnam. Assigned FSN 6920-716-2351, they came packaged in a carton of ten rolls of 500 pasters each. . . . .$10-12 box

Black pasters were used to repair other areas of the targets. Each 5,000-count box contained ten rolls of FSN 6920-716-2350 pasters. . . . .$10-12 box

Another version of the black paster was the FSN 6920-716-2359. . . . .$10-12 box

To clean the M14, the brush FSN 1005-690-8441 was used. These brushes were an important part of every GI's gear in the early stages of the Vietnam War. . . . . $20-25 per box

Every GI issued an M14 was also issued this cleaning kit. $25-30

ARMY: ORDNANCE CORPS

During the initial fielding of the M16, the weapons developed a terrible reputation for jamming. This was (erroneously) blamed on the guns not being properly cleaned, so these kits were expedited to troops in the field with rifle-specific cleaning instructions. Note the smaller diameter jointed cleaning rod and improved chamber-cleaning brush in the background. $25-30

Warman's Vietnam War Collectibles Identification and Price Guide

Standard issue "Case, Small Arms Accessories" for the primary components of the issue M16 cleaning kit: A simple envelope made of vinyl material to carry the jointed cleaning rod, oiler and brushes. $5-10

This oil bottle was a key component of every M16 rifleman's gear. . . $2-3

These cotton patches were also important to keeping the weapons operating properly. They were packed 200 per box, with FSN 1005-288-3565. As with many small items of this nature, the real value as a collectible comes from the Vietnam-dated packaging. $5-10

The standard Army cleaning patch was too large for the .223-caliber M16, so a smaller patch, FSN 1005-912-4248, was developed. $9-12

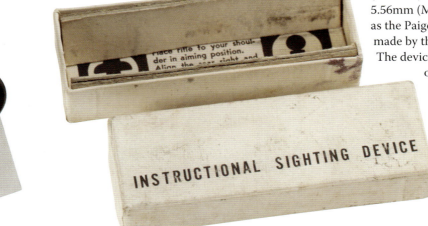

This marksmanship training aid was intended for use with .30-caliber (7.62mm) M1, M1 Carbine, M14 and 5.56mm (M16) weapons. Known as the Paige sighting device, it was made by the Paige Co. in New York. The device has a soft wood spindle of two diameters that is inserted into the rifle muzzle and holds an adjustable and proportional-size target to simulate the correct sight picture to the recruit in primary marksmanship training. $25-35

ARMY: ORDNANCE CORPS

This is the detachable bipod and its carrier case for the M16. It was designated "Bipod, Rifle, M3 W/ Carrying Case." The lightweight aluminum spring-loaded device was intended to assist accurate firing in the sustained-fire role. **$10-15**

This is a seven-unit carton of 20-round magazines for the M16. The FSN for each magazine was 1005-056-2237. Some collectors believe a premium should be added for the Vietnam-dated carton. **$150-200**

New magazines sometimes came packed in weather-resistant packaging, as seen by this Feb. 1963 magazine for the 7.62 mm M-14. . **$20-40**

Magazines in sealed GI packaging bring premium prices. As a rule, 20-round magazines made prior to 1969 are marked "CAL. .223" and beginning in 1970 the magazines were marked "CAL. 5.56MM." Both Colt and Simmonds made these magazines, with Simmonds being much scarcer. **$20-40**

This trooper, maintaining perimeter in Vietnam in January 1970, has laid out several bandoleers of ammunition for his M16A1. Lying on one bandoleer is the trigger for a Claymore mine, and four M26-type grenades are also visible. National Archives photo.

A bandoleer of M16 ammunition consisted of a seven-pocket bandoleer, 14 10-round stripper clips loaded with ammo that were packed into seven cardboard sleeves. One magazine filler was furnished with each bandoleer. Priced here with ammunition.................. $50-100

M16 ammunition was supplied separately to the troops. Stripper clips, each holding ten rounds, were placed on the magazine using a feeder, and then the rounds were forced into the magazine. Magazine feeder and stripper clips have about the same value............................$3-5

ARMY: ORDNANCE CORPS

Ammunition for the ARVN M-1 Garand .30-caliber weapons was supplied in this type bandoleers. Each bandoleer held six eight-round clips. Priced bandoleer alone. $5-10

The 7.62 ammunition for the M14 also came in a cloth bandoleer. $5-10

This is the ammunition bag or bandoleer for the M60 medium machine gun. The metal-linked 7.62mm NATO ammunition for the M60 came packed in a heavy-duty "30 Cal." waterproof metal box, of the same dimensions as the WWII .30-caliber machine gun ammo, with four cans per wood and wire-bound crate. Each M60 ammo can contains 200 rounds of linked ammunition, two belts of 100 rounds each per can. Each 100-round belt is packed in a thin tan cardboard box that is inserted into this disposable cotton carrying bag. The long web piece is the "one size fits all" shoulder strap. The web strap is adjusted for carrying with a large heavy-duty, black-painted brass safety pin that came with the each bag, the same pin as with the rifle ammunition bandoleers. After the ammunition was expended, the safety pins were a handy item that the GI's could retain for a million other uses. The bag is printed in black block letters with the ammunition description and specific lot number of the ammunition for identification. $10-15

Warman's Vietnam War Collectibles Identification and Price Guide

The M1911A1 was fed .45-caliber ACP ammo from a seven-round magazine. Look for the FSN and an appropriately dated contract number **$10-40**

This is the Web Sling M1 that replaced the two-piece M1907 Leather model used on rifles through WWII. The simplified M1 Web Sling was introduced in the late 1940s. It was designed to fit several weapons, including the M1 Garand and others, then carried over to the M14 and then to the M16. This one is interesting because of the Vietnam-era date on the packing label, which confirms its later manufacture. **$10-15**

This folding tripod supported a sniper's spotting scope. Made of lightweight aluminum, the low-profile M15 folding tripod fitted with the M49 high-power spotting telescopes could be used in stationary observation posts for enemy observation, artillery adjustment and perimeter defense. They were standard sniper equipment issue in Vietnam when unit sniper schools were expanded in country. The tripod was carried in a canvas M42A1 case and is still in use today............................. **$50-60**

ARMY: Ordnance Corps

The M49 is a 20-power daytime telescope. It has a field of view of 2 degrees 12 minutes. This has been the army's standard observation telescope from 1944 through today, and is currently assigned NSN: 6650-00-678-5627. The scope came in a plastic M164 case with web strap. Later models use nylon straps, while the WWII-era telescope came in a leather case. **$250-300**

Warman's Vietnam War Collectibles Identification and Price Guide

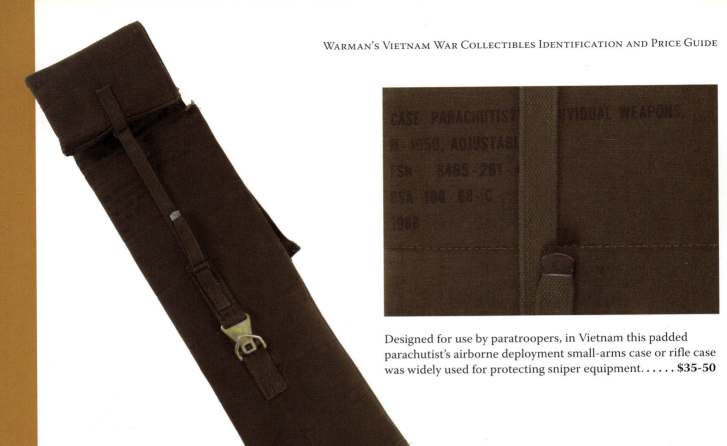

Designed for use by paratroopers, in Vietnam this padded parachutist's airborne deployment small-arms case or rifle case was widely used for protecting sniper equipment. $35-50

Grenades

The M26, and its successor, the M26A1, shown here, were first used in Korea. Like the pineapple, these grenades were also extensively used by U.S. troops from the early stages of the Vietnam War. Price shown is for a genuine inert grenade. Cast-steel dummy replicas are widely available for about $5-8. . . . . $40-60

The classic MK-II "pineapple" grenade went to Vietnam with the first U.S. troops in the country. This was to be last large-scale use of the WWII-era piece of ordnance. The grenades were packed in cardboard tubes. Price shown is for a genuine inert grenade. Cast-steel dummy replicas are widely available for about $5-8. . . . . $40-60

The "baseball" grenade, the M67, was the final fragmentation grenade issued to U.S. troops in Vietnam. Lighter than its predecessors, it was hoped this would give troops using it the ability to throw it farther. This style of grenade remains in use with U.S. forces today. Price shown is for a genuine inert grenade. Cast-steel dummy replicas are widely available for about $5-8. . . . . $40-60

ARMY: ORDNANCE CORPS

This is the M18A1 Claymore antipersonnel mine system. This consists of the above-ground mine, a detonator, test set and the electric blasting cap assembly M4. The rubber-covered, two-wire coil is used in connected from the mine to the remote hand-held detonator assembly. The object with the plastic dust cap is the connector that plugs into the detonator. The complete system came packed in a cloth bag, shown below, with instructions sewn inside of it.

We should note that there is a Practice Claymore Mine Set M-68 that sometimes comes onto the collector market. These are identical to the live munitions except that the inert training mine is identified by being a light blue color. Some collectors have reconfigured these practice sets for display by repainting the inert blue-color Claymore to standard Olive Drab.

Collectors should be aware when performing public displays it is best that such items be labeled as "Empty, Inert, Safe and Harmless" and are for instructional historic display only. The value listed below is for the practice set, or the M18A1 that has been professionally rendered inert. $75-125

Knives and Bayonets

The M4 bayonet was designed for use with the M1 Carbine, many of which were supplied to Vietnamese forces. M4s produced after 1954 have plastic, rather than leather grips, the leather tending to deteriorate in the tropics.
.... $30-40

The M5A1 was an improved M5, which had been introduced in 1955 for use with the famed M1 Garand. As with the Garand itself, many of these bayonets were supplied to the Army of the Republic of Vietnam by the United States. The example shown here was made by Milpar. The M5 and M5A1 were used with the M8A1 scabbard.................................. $30-40

ARMY: Ordnance Corps

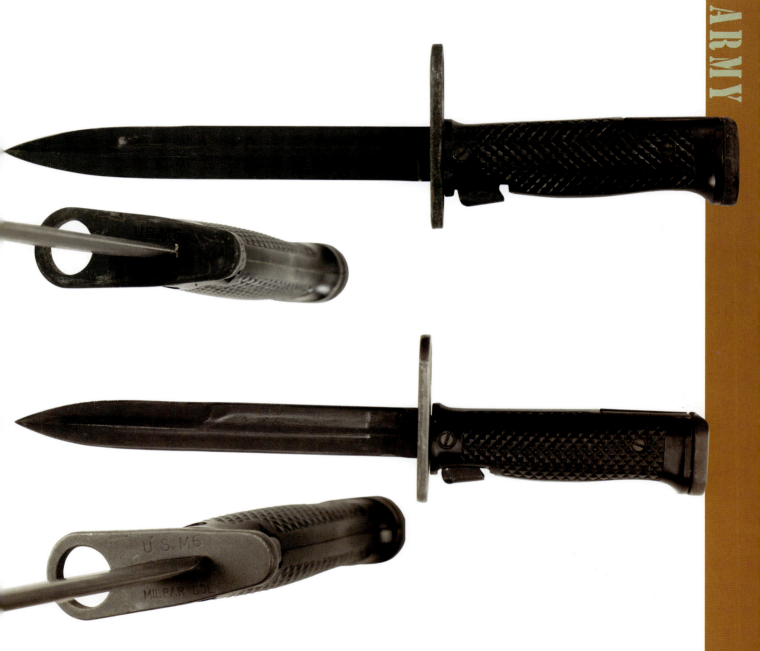

The M6 was derived from the M5A1, and was designed for use with the M14. The method of attaching the bayonet differed, with the M5A1's unique gas plug locking system being replaced with a traditional muzzle-ring system. Makers marks found on the M6 include Aerial Cutlery, Imperial Knife and Columbus Milpar & Mfg. This bayonet was issued with the M8A1 scabbard. $30-40

The M7 bayonet was made by a variety of manufacturers. From left to right in this photo are M7 bayonets made by Ontario, Milpar, Imperial and Bauer, respectively. The Ontario, Imperial and Bauer Ord bayonets have the originally specified style of runout, while the Milpar M7 is shown with the later-style tapered runout. Authentic Vietnam-era Colt M7 bayonets command even higher prices than the ones listed here.

Maker marks for the bayonet are typically found on the underside of the guard, and usually include the designation "M7," as does this example made by Ontario Knife Co.
.... **$15-20**

Columbus Milpar and Manufacturing was one of the Army's major suppliers of the M7, and examples marked Milpar are easily located. Some unassembled Milpar parts were sold surplus at the end of the contract, and have since been used in combination with new parts from other manufacturers to forge a number of different types of bayonets.
.... **$10-15**

Bauer Ordnance Co. of Detroit produced about 1.75 million M7 bayonets on a 1969 contract, making this one of the most common variations. Brand-new, unissued examples sealed in their original packing can still be found on the market. **$20-35**

ARMY: ORDNANCE CORPS

MECHANIZED

> **MILITARY VEHICLES CRITERIA**
> 1. **Excellent:** Restored to maximum professional standards or a near-perfect original.
> 2. **Fine:** Well restored or a combination of superior reproduction and excellent original parts.
> 3. **Very good:** Complete and operable original, or older restoration, or very good amateur restoration with all presentable and serviceable parts inside and out.
> 4. **Good:** Functional or needs minor work to be functional. Also, a deteriorated restoration or poor amateur restoration.
> 5. **Restorable:** Needs complete restoration to body, chassis and interior. May or may not be running, but is not wrecked, weathered or stripped.
> 6. **Parts vehicle:** Deteriorated beyond the point of restoration.

Photo courtesy of Verne Kindischi

M41 WALKER BULLDOG

Named in honor of General W.W. Walker, the M41 Walker Bulldog succeeded the M24 Chaffee as the U.S. Army's light reconnaissance tank in the late 1950s. The M41's Continental air-cooled, 6-cylinder, opposed and supercharged gasoline engine made it among the last U.S. armored vehicles to be gasoline fueled. The AOS-895 originally installed was carbureted, but later versions were fuel injected to improve the vehicle's range. M41s and M41A1s powered with the fuel-injected engines were M41A2 and M41A3, respectively.

The engine and transmission were rear-mounted, with the driver's position in the bow. The Bulldog rode on torsion-bar suspension, as did most post-WWII U.S. tanks. The Bulldog's main gun was the 76mm M32. The installation of a bore evacuator, which cleared the gun tube after firing, was a first for a U.S. tank. The large bustle at the rear of the turret housed both the radio gear and a large ventilation fan, and also acted as a counterweight balance for the main gun. Intended for fast reconnaissance, the Bulldog's primary defense was flight. Its light armor could not stand up to tank-on-tank duels, nor was its main gun well suited for such engagements.

Over 3,700 M41 series Light Tanks were built, and Cadillac Motors of GM was the primary manufacturer. The M41 was not used by U.S. Forces in Vietnam, but several examples were provided to the ARVN.

Weight . . . . 51,800 lbs
Size (LxWxH) . . . . 323.375 x 126 x 112
Max Speed . . . . 45 mph
Armament . . . . **76mm cannon, 1 x .30, 1 x .50-caliber machine guns**

6	5	4	3	2	1
$25,000	$35,000	$45,000	$55,000	$70,000	$80,000

National Archives photo

M551 SHERIDAN

The M551 Sheridan is immediately recognized for its role in Vietnam. Less publicized was its successful use during Desert Storm.

Designed to be a light reconnaissance tank, the M551 combined amphibious and airborne assault capabilities with a powerful main gun.

The 152mm Gun/Launcher could fire either conventional ammunition or the Shillelagh anti-tank missile. The vehicle was designed primarily as a missile launcher, so when firing conventional munitions, the recoil of the big gun was tremendous, lifting the front of the lightweight vehicle from the ground.

Although the turret, usually the easiest target for enemy gunners, was made of conventional steel armor, the Sheridan's hull was made of welded 7039 aluminum alloy armor plate. This was done to keep the vehicle's weight low in conjunction with its role in airborne and amphibious assaults. The hull was enclosed in high-density foam to improve floatation, and a second layer of aluminum was added all around to form the exterior surfaces. During their service, the M551 had updated gun-laying systems installed. These vehicles were then classified M551A1.

The Allison Division of General Motors built 1,562 of these tanks beginning in 1966.

Withdrawn from frontline services without a replacement after Desert Storm, some are in use at the desert-training center masquerading as Soviet vehicles.

Weight . . . .**33,460 lbs**
Size (LxWxH) . . . . **248.3 x 110 x 150**
Max Speed . . . . **45 mph**
Armament . . . . **152mm Gun/Launcher, 1 x .30, 1 x .50-caliber machine guns.**

6	5	4	3	2	1
$25,000	$35,000	$45,000	$55,000	$70,000	$80,000

ARMY: ORDNANCE CORPS

Photo courtesy of the Don F. Pratt Museum, Ft. Campbell, Ky.

M48A2 PATTON

The M48 was an outgrowth of M26/46 Pershing series of tanks, with the M47 as a stopgap until the new M48, initially the T48, could be fully developed. The M48 was produced in a variety of models. The most noteworthy of these is the M48A2, which was America's main tank in Vietnam.

The M48A2 introduced a fuel-injected engine to the series, which increased range significantly. The new power pack had relocated oil coolers, which increased space available in the engine compartment and allowed larger fuel tanks to either side. This also brought about an improved engine deck of the M48A2 design to accommodate these changes. The new design eliminated the majority of the tank's infrared signature. The exhaust was no longer directed out the top of the rear deck, but instead was routed through two large louvered doors at the rear of the hull. This rear-armor design remained basically unchanged through the rest of this series, as well as the M60 Patton series. Most M48A2s have three return rollers rather than the five per each side on earlier models. An exception appears to be Marine Corps vehicles, which evidently kept the five-roller system.

The M48A2 and its subtypes were produced in greater abundance than any of the others, and remained in production until 1959. A later variation of the M48A2 was known as the M48A2C. The M48A2C had a coincidence range finder rather than the troublesome stereoscopic range finder of earlier models.

Weight	105,000 pounds
Size (LxWxH)	342 x 143.5 x 121.875
Max Speed	30 mph
Armament	90mm Gun M41, 1x.30/1x.50

6	5	4	3	2	1
$30,000	$40,000	$60,000	$66,000	$80,000	$90,000

National Archives photo.

THE M113

The shape of this vehicle has become readily identifiable as American armored personnel carrier. This is largely due to the long service life of it and its variants. The M113 has been the Army's standard APC since production began at Food Machinery Corp. (FMC) in 1960.

The hull of the M113 vehicles is made of aluminum armor. A hydraulically operated ramp in the rear allows rapidly loading and unloading of troops, while a personnel door allows crew access. The driver's position was in the left front, and the power plant was to the driver's right. The driver was provided with four M17 periscopes, and his hatch had provision for a M19 infrared periscope as well. The commander's station is behind the driver and power plant, and he had a cupola equipped with five M17 periscopes and a M2 HB machine gun. There were provisions for 11 passengers to ride in the carrier. An unusual feature of the M113 was the hydraulically tensioned track, rather than the usual hand-adjusted track of other armored vehicles. The M113 was amphibious, being propelled in the water by its tracks. However, there was only 14 inches of freeboard when the vehicle was in the water.

A Chrysler 75M V-8 engine driving through an Allison TX200-2 engine powered the M113. There were 4,974 M113s built for the U.S. Armed Forces, and 9,839 supplied to other countries.

Weight . . . . 20,310 pounds
Size (LxWxH) . . . . 191.5 x 105.75 x 98.25
Max Speed . . . . 40 mph
Range, Land . . . . 200 miles

6	5	4	3	2	1
$6,000	$10,000	$14,000	$19,000	$25,000	$40,000

ARMY: ORDNANCE CORPS

U.S. Army photo.

THE M113A1

The ink was hardly dry on the initial production contracts for the M113 when work began on a diesel-powered version. After trials of various versions, a version powered by the General Motors 6V53 V-6 diesel engine was standardized as M113A1 in May 1963, with production beginning the following year. The V-6 diesel's power was transmitted to the track through an Allison TX-100 automatic transmission and a DS-200 controlled differential.

This version of the M113 was used extensively in Vietnam, where the VC dubbed it the "green dragon." It was in Vietnam that the concept of the Infantry Fighting Vehicle really began to come into its own. Having early on been provided with a few of these APCs, the ARVN began to fight from the vehicle, rather than simply using it as a taxi. In addition to the commander's .50-caliber machine gun, troopers also fought from the top hatches in the cargo area. After 14 .50 cal gunners were lost at the Battle of Ap Bac in January 1963, work began to provide some degree of armor protection for the exposed gun positions.

Food Machinery Corp. (FMC) designed a circular gun shield for the commander's .50-caliber that could be added to his cupola. Additionally, shielded mounts for two 7.62 mm M60 machine guns, one either side of the rear hatch, were installed. Vehicles so modified were referred to as the M113 Armored Cavalry vehicle (ACAV). In addition to a driver and its commander, the ACAV was crewed by two M60 gunners and two loaders. One of the loaders had a M79 40mm grenade launcher

Weight . . . . 21,474 pounds
Size (LxWxH) . . . . 191.5 x 105.75 x 98.25
Max Speed . . . . 37 mph
Range . . . . 300 miles

6	5	4	3	2	1
$6,000	$10,000	$14,000	$19,000	$25,000	$40,000

M106 107MM SELF-PROPELLED MORTAR

The M106 was essentially a M113 with a round roof hatch through which the rear-firing mortar, which was mounted below on a 90-degree traversing mechanism, fired. The mortar, the 107mm M30, was originally classified as the 4.2" mortar M30, but was redesignated when the U.S. Army adopted the metric system.

Procurement of the Chrysler gas-engine-powered M106 began even before the type had been standardized. Of the 860 units Food Machinery Corp. (FMC) built, 589 went to U.S. forces, the balance to overseas sales.

When production of the base M113 vehicles changed from gasoline-engine-driven units to diesel-powered machines, so did the mortar carrier, becoming the M106A1. The U.S. military received 982 of these, with a further 334 provided for overseas sales.

When the M113A1 was again upgraded, becoming the M113A2, the M106 followed suit, getting the same upgrades and becoming the M106A2.

A base plate for the mortar was stowed on the rear outer left side of the hull, allowing the weapon to be removed from the vehicle and fired.

Weight . . . . 26,000 pounds
Size (LxWxH) . . . . 194 x 112.75 x 98.25
Max Speed . . . . 37 mph
Range . . . . 300 miles

6	5	4	3	2	1
$25,000	$35,000	$45,000	$55,000	$70,000	$80,000

ARMORED COMMAND AND RECONNAISSANCE CARRIER

Though the M114 somewhat resembles the M113, the 114 is not an armored personnel carrier at all. Rather, its intended role was more closely aligned with that of the WWII-era M3A1 and M8 armored cars—to probe for enemy forces, radio their position, and beat a hasty retreat once contact was made.

Unfortunately, its off-road performance was not adequate to this task. Particularly deplorable was the fact that the hull extended forward of the tracks, causing the bow to dig in when crossing obstacles, immobilizing the carrier. The Cadillac-built vehicle was fully amphibious and air-transportable. Water propulsion was provided by its shrouded tracks. With its low profile, there was only space for the three-man crew of driver, commander, observer and a single passenger inside the M114. Power was provided by a Chevy 283 V-8 engine and Hydramatic transmission. It rode on torsion-bar suspension.

On early models, the commander had a cupola with an externally mounted .50-caliber machine gun, while on later models this was replaced by a turret-type arrangement. The observer had a hatch on the right side of the hull, just rear of the commander's position. The observer was provided with two pedestal mounts for his machine gun. A large circular door was located in the rear wall of the hull.

The M114A1, the most numerous of the series, had a turret-type machine gun mount on the hull roof. Production of the lightweight, aluminum-armored vehicle began in 1962, and the last variants were retired in the early 1980s.

Weight . . . . 14,749 pounds
Size (LxWxH) . . . . 175.75 x 91.75 x 91.125
Max Speed . . . . 40 mph
Range . . . . 300 miles

6	5	4	3	2	1
$6,000	$10,000	$14,000	$19,000	$25,000	$40,000

ARMY: ORDNANCE CORPS

U.S. Army photo.

M116 HUSKY

By the late 1950s, the newest Weasel was nearing 15 years old, and a program to create its replacement was undertaken. The Pacific Car and Foundry Co. (PCF) designed the Husky for this purpose, and built four pilot and three preproduction models by 1961. After testing, and a few recommended modifications, the vehicle was designated the M116 and a contract was issued for the vehicle to be placed in production. Surprisingly, the Blaw-Knox Co., famed for building huge radio antennas and construction equipment, won the bid to build the 197 production units. Pacific wasn't out of the fight yet, and it won contracts to build 111 of the M116A1 for the Navy and Marine Corps.

The Chevrolet V8 with Hydramatic transmission power plant was positioned behind the driver. Its cooling air was drawn through a grille in the roof, and exhaust passed through a grille on the right side of the vehicle.

A hinged door in the rear of the hull provided entrance and exit to the cargo space, and a winch was mounted on the front of the vehicle. The cargo area floor was moveable and could be raised to provide a flat cargo floor or lowered to provide troop seats. A canvas cargo cover and bows could cover the cargo space, or a hard winter top could be mounted.

The Husky had a welded aluminum hull and fiberglass cab for light weight.

The Husky had a load rating of 1-1/2 tons on both land and water and was propelled by its spinning tracks.

Weight . . . . .10,600 lbs
Size (LxWxH) . . . . 188 x 82 x 79
Max Speed Land . . . . 37 mph
Max Speed Water . . . . 4.2 mph
Range . . . . 300 miles

6	5	4	3	2	1
$3,500	$8,500	$14,000	$18,000	$22,000	$28,000

U.S. Army photo.

M548 CARRIER

Originally developed for the Signal Corps as a carrier for radar systems, the M548 went on to be used in a variety of roles. Among these was ammunition carrier for the M107, M108, M109, and M110 self-propelled artillery pieces, as well as a Lance missile carrier.

Although one can hardly tell from appearances, the M548 was built using automotive components of the M113A1 family of vehicles. Hence, as improvements were made in the M113A1, similar improvements were made to the M548. And, as the M113A1 was upgraded to M113A2, the same changes were applied to the M538, resulting in the M548A1. In addition, the M548A1 had a 1,500-pound-capacity chain hoist added in the cargo compartment.

Later, as the 6V53T turbo-supercharged engine and Allison X200-4 cross-drive transmission were added to the M113, resulting in the M113A3, some of the M548A1 were similarly upgraded. These changes not only made driver training easier, but also made the carrier's performance equal to that of the Army's frontline fighting equipment

Weight . . . . .28,300 lbs
Size (LxWxH) . . . . 232 x 105.75 x 110.75
Max Speed land. . . . . 35 mph
Range . . . . 300 miles

6	5	4	3	2	1
$4,500	$10,000	$15,000	$20,000	$23,000	$28,000

ARMY: Ordnance Corps

National Archives Photo

M42 DUSTER

As tank chassis evolved, so did support vehicles built on tank chassis. The M42 was the successor to the M19, and like the M19 was armed with dual automatic Bofors 40mm anti-aircraft cannon. The earliest production vehicles had conical-shaped, naval-style flash suppressors on the gun muzzles, but later production vehicles used a three-prong type. A 30-caliber machine gun was pintle-mounted on the side of the turret for close-in defense.

A six-man crew served the Duster. The driver and commander rode in the hull, and a four-man gun crew rode in the open-topped turret. The gun crew was comprised of a sight setter, a gunner and two loaders to feed the voracious appetite of the weapon.

When fuel injection was added to the AOS-895-5 engine, the vehicles affected were classified as M42A1.

With the speed of aircraft increasing, the usefulness of the Duster as an anti-aircraft weapon became questionable. However, during the Vietnam conflict, the Duster, with its twin Bofors cannons, were employed effectively against enemy troop formations. Even in dense jungle, the heavy 40mm shell was devastating, as it also was in urban settings.

Weight . . . . .49,500 lbs
Size (LxWxH) . . . . .250 x 127 x 112
Max Speed . . . . 45 mph
Range 100

6	5	4	3	2	1
$9,000	$14,000	$20,000	$26,000	$35,000	$45,000

M55 8-INCH SELF-PROPELLED HOWITZER AND M53 155MM SELF-PROPELLED GUN

Styled similar to the smaller M52 105mm Self-Propelled Howitzer, the M55 shown here was one of the largest U.S. vehicles fielded in Vietnam.

Though its engine and transmission were located in the front of the vehicle, the M55 was nonetheless based on the automotive components of the M48 tank. Pacific Car and Foundry (PCF), the vehicle's builder, used both the AV-1790-7B engine and CD-850-4B transmission to simplify logistics. The large turret at the rear of the M53 housed a 155mm cannon, while the M55 mounted an 8-inch howitzer.

Since they used the same chassis, many M53s were converted to M55s during the Vietnam War.

Weight . . . . .98,000 lbs
Size (LxWxH) . . . . .311 x 133 x 137
Max Speed . . . . 30 mph
Armament . . . . 1 x 8-inch howitzer

6	5	4	3	2	1
$7,000	$15,000	$25,000	$35,000	$45,000	$60,000

ARMY: ORDNANCE CORPS

U.S. Army photo.

M56 SCORPION

One of the most unusual looking vehicles fielded by the Army was the M56 Scorpion. Cadillac began building the M56 in 1957 at its Cleveland tank plant. Ultimately, 325 of the self-propelled anti-tank guns rolled off the line. Armed with a 90mm gun, and manned by a crew of four, the Scorpion was intended to be an air-mobile anti-tank weapon.

The lightweight and basic design of the M56 omitted weather protection for the four-man crew. To the left of the manually elevated and traversed main gun was the driver's station and controls, with a windshield incorporated in the gun splinter shield. To the driver's left was the radio equipment, which formed the base of the commander's seat. The other two crew members rode on the other side of the breech.

The hull of the vehicle was of aluminum construction, with the splinter shield the only real armor on the vehicle.

A Continental six-cylinder, horizontally opposed gasoline engine powered the Scorpion. Its running gear was unusual in that it featured pneumatic tires on the four road wheels on each side. In U.S. service, the Scorpion was used by the 82nd and 101st Airborne Divisions only from 1957 until 1970, including service in Vietnam.

The big gun, however, was deemed too powerful for the light chassis, as the recoil lifted the front of the vehicle off the ground.

Weight . . . . 15,500 lbs
Size (LxWxH) . . . . 230 x 101.5 x 81
Max Speed . . . . 28 mph
Armament . . . . 90mm Gun M54

6	5	4	3	2	1
$6,500	$9,000	$14,000	$20,000	$26,000	$35,000

U.S. Army photo.

M107 175MM SELF-PROPELLED GUN

Pacific Car and Foundry (PCF) began delivering the M107 in 1962. These vehicles, and others on the same chassis, played a prominent role in Vietnam. Though self-propelled, the chassis with the big gun could scarcely be considered mobile. Its 13-man crew would establish a fire-base, place the weapon, and thus command the battlefield for a 20-mile radius.

The rotating gun was mounted at the rear of the open vehicle. The mount could be rotated 30 degrees either side of center, and the gun elevated to 65 degrees. A spade at the rear of the hull anchored the vehicle during firing. In later years, both Food Machinery Corp. (FMC) and Bowen-McLaughlin-York (BMY) produced the M107.

Regardless of who built them, the M107s, with their incredibly long gun tubes, were unmistakable.

Weight . . . . .62,100 lbs
Size (LxWxH) . . . . 444.8 x 124 x 136.8
Max Speed . . . . 34 mph
Armament . . . . 175mm Gun M113

6	5	4	3	2	1
$7,000	$15,000	$25,000	$35,000	$45,000	$60,000

ARMY: Ordnance Corps

U.S. Army photo.

M110 8-INCH HOWITZER

The M110 8-inch Howitzer was produced concurrently with the M107, with which it shared a chassis. Like the M107, the M110 also was originally built by Pacific Car and Foundry (PCF), and later Food Machinery Corp. (FMC) and Bowen-McLaughlin-York (BMY).

Torsion-bar suspension equipped with five dual rubber-tired road wheels on each side supported the vehicle. The drive sprocket was at the front and the fifth road wheel acted as the idler. The return run of track ran out top of the road wheels. The vehicles were powered by a Detroit Diesel Model 8V-71T diesel engine driving through an Allison XTG-411-2A cross-drive transmission at the front of the hull.

The M110 was used extensively in Vietnam. Though its range was only about half that of the M107, its 200-pound round had a reputation for greater accuracy and ease of use than did the 175mm round.

```
Weight . . . . . . . . . . . . . . . . . . . . . . . . . . . . . . . . . . .58,500 lbs
Size (LxWxH) . . . . . . . . . . . . . . . . . . . . 294.4 x 124 x 115.6
Max Speed . . . . . . . . . . . . . . . . . . . . . . . . . . . . . . . . 34 mph
Armament . . . . . . . . . . . . . . . . . . . . . . .8" Howitzer M2A2
```

Not available on the collector market

U.S. Army photo.

M109A1 SELF-PROPELLED HOWITZER

The big gun, fully enclosed turret and tracks lead many casual observers to believe this vehicle is a tank. In reality, however, it is self-propelled artillery, and its armor is of little use against anything more substantial than an infantryman's rifle.

Development of this family of vehicles began in the late 1950s. Early on, there was a M108 variant that was armed with a 105mm howitzer, but it was soon discontinued in favor of its companion vehicle, the 155mm howitzer armed M109. Production of both vehicles began in 1962. Production of the M108 ended in 1963, while production of the M109 continued until 1969. All the M109s were built in the Cleveland tank plant, but depending upon the contract and year of manufacture, the builders were Cadillac Motor Car division of General Motors, Chrysler Corp., and Allison Division of General Motors.

The Army bought 1,961 M109s, while the Marines bought 150 more. Though not as often photographed in country as were the open-topped M107 and M110, the M109s were deployed to Vietnam. It was there that it was learned that the T255E4 155mm weapon mounted in the vehicle, when firing the XM1119 propelling charge for maximum range, caused serious damage to both the vehicle and its crew.

Installing the longer barreled M185 howitzer solved this problem. Very little modification to the vehicle was necessary to accomplish this, with the end result being the M109A1. In 1972 mass conversion of the M109 fleet into the M109A1 configuration began.

Bowen-McLaughlin-York began producing a factory-fresh M109A1 from scratch in 1974.

Weight . . . . .53,060 lbs
Size (LxWxH) . . . . 356.3 x 124 x 129.1
Max Speed . . . . 35 mph
Armament . . . . . **155mm Howitzer M185, 1 x .50 M2 HB Machine Gun**

Not available on the collector market

ARMY: ORDNANCE CORPS

U.S. Army photo.

M88 TANK RECOVERY VEHICLE

As the size and weight of America's tanks increased, it became evident that even the improved M74 would not be up to the task. In 1959, production of the M88 began by Bowen-McLaughlin-York Inc. of York, Pa., which had also designed the vehicle. The initial order was for 1,075 vehicles. Their design has proven to be well thought out and durable.

The M88 is built on an armored chassis similar to a tank, and shares many components with the M48/M60 Medium Tank families. The lower portion of the hull is filled with two hydraulically powered winches, a hoist winch and a separate main winch. The 50,000-pound capacity hoist winch uses an A-frame boom and 400 feet of 5/8-inch wire rope for heavy lifting. The main recovery winch has a 90,000-pound capacity and its drum holds 200 feet of 1.25-inch wire rope.

Other hydraulically operated equipment includes a bow-mounted blade, boom, refueling pump and a powerful impact wrench. The front-mounted bulldozer blade is used to hold and stabilize the retriever during heavy lifting and for all winching operations.

Weight . . . . **112,000 lbs**
Size (LxWxH) . . . . **325.5 x 135 x 115**
Max Speed . . . . **30 mph**
Range . . . . **222 miles**

Not readily available.

This photo of SP4 Steven Paffel, Team 22, Company H (Ranger) 75th Infantry Regiment, along the Dong Nai River in 1970, exhibits precisely why the traditional leather U.S. combat boot did not fare well in Vietnam. The constant exposure to moisture simply rotted the stitching away. This led to the development of an array of specialized footwear during the war. Specialist Paffel is about to load his M79 grenade launcher. National Archives Photo.

Quartermaster Corps

The U.S. military is organized so that it is almost self-contained. The objective is to be able to keep an army of thousands of men in the field operating independently of local supplies of any type of material. Much of this material—food, clothing, petroleum products among them—are the responsibility of the Quartermaster Corps.

The Second Continental Congress established the position of Quartermaster General on June 16, 1775. The Quartermaster Corps proper was created by Congress in 1912 by merging the Subsistence, Pay and Quartermaster departments. The responsibility of the Quartermaster Corps in Vietnam was to provide supplies needed by the individual combat soldier in the field.

ARMY: QUARTERMASTER CORPS

In this section of the book are grouped the items typically supplied by the Quartermaster Corps for use by Army personnel in the field. Specialized items used by MP, Medics, etc., are found in their respective sections. Within the Quartermaster section of this book, the collectibles are further broken down by type, such as headgear, uniforms, rations, etc. Of note to collectors, most Quartermaster items did not have cut-and-dried dates for changes to equipment. Rather, similar items were often produced in overlapping periods, with both an "old" and a "new" specification at the same time.

BOOTS

During the Vietnam War a variety of footwear was distributed and worn by U.S. forces. The "classic" footwear was the jungle boot. Development of what was to become the jungle boot began in 1955, with the intent to eliminate a longstanding problem with U.S. combat boots. At least as far back as WWII, the army had experienced problems with the stitching in conventional boots deteriorating rapidly when worn in tropical environments.

www.vietnamgear.com

www.vietnamgear.com

JUNGLE BOOTS DMS
The Tropical Combat Boot was a considerable improvement over its predecessors, but was far from ideal. The extremely moist and hot conditions of the tropics brought about stitching failure at the sole. Sometimes these failures could occur after only one month of service. Hence, the Direct Molded Sole (DMS) began to be used. In this manufacturing technique, the sole was vulcanized to the upper rather than stitched to it. The uppers of these boots were made from nylon duck and leather, and laced all the way up, rather than using a combination of laces and buckles. Both the top stay as well as the backstay were leather-reinforced. On the inside arch of each boot were a pair of screened brass drainage eyelets countersunk into the boot...**$125-175**

TROPICAL COMBAT BOOTS
The earliest of the U.S. jungle boots featured canvas uppers, and two buckle fasteners held the boot to the leg. These fasteners were among the shortcomings of this boot style, as they became entangled in the dense undergrowth found in Southeast Asia. **$150-200**

In 1965, BATA began to manufacture a second style of jungle boot for the Army. These boots differed from the earlier pattern by having the top and back stays reinforced with 1-inch wide nylon webbing rather than leather. Additionally, the brass drainage eyelets were surface mounted instead of being countersunk. $40-60

ARMY: Quartermaster Corps

JUNGLE BOOTS DMS SPIKE PROTECTIVE

Punji sticks, made of wood or bamboo, and often deliberately contaminated with feces, poisons, etc., were frequently encountered in Vietnam. VC favored these simple, inexpensive booby traps because so many assets were required to extricate the wounded soldier, who faced a painful and prolonged recovery period.

In October 1961, in an effort to defend U.S. troops against this type of weapon, Natick Laboratories set out to develop a spike-resistant insole insert for use with the jungle boot. This insole is described in detail elsewhere in this chapter. However, the insert was not entirely satisfactory, and accordingly, Natick began developing a boot with integral spike protection, with the design finalized in May 1966. This boot featured a two-inch wide ankle support, and one-inch wide reinforcements of top and backstays, both made of nylon webbing. Like all the jungle boots before it, this boot had a mountaineering-inspired Vibram tread pattern.

www.vietnamgear.com

JUNGLE BOOTS DMS SPIKE PROTECTIVE, PANAMA SOLE

The mud prevalent in tropical conditions tended to cake into the tread of the Vibram soles, making the boots heavy and traction poor. As early as 1944, this problem was recognized by the Army, and in that year technicians of the Army's Panama Mobile Force created a tread pattern that would counter this difficulty. However, this pattern was not officially tested until 1967. Following field testing in 1968, the Army Materiel Command directed the "new" type sole be used on all Tropical Combat Boots. The military specification MIL-B-43154 was changed accordingly. The boot retained the spike protection found in its immediate predecessor. In May 1972 the official nomenclature of the boot became Boot, Hot Weather, Men's. $40-60

LEATHER COMBAT BOOTS

Though iconic, the jungle boot was not the only type used by the U.S. Army in Vietnam. Black leather combat boots were used prior to, and even after, the adoption of the jungle boot. In most instances, the problem with the leather combat boot was the stitching in the leather soles, which did not hold up well in the tropics. However, troops exposed to a significant fire hazard (such as helicopter crewmen) were issued the leather boots nonetheless. The danger of the nylon in the jungle boot melting and causing serious injury in the event of fire outweighed the cost of the frequent repair of the leather boots. **$20-40**

LEATHER COMBAT BOOTS, DIRECT MOLDED SOLE

Ultimately, a leather boot was developed that had a direct molded sole. The sole of these shoes had a distinctive Chevron tread pattern. Procurement of this style boot began in the summer of 1964, although it was not classified as standard "A" until January 1967. In addition to having a longer life, these boots also weighed less than the stitched-sole version................................... **$50-75**

MEDICAL DEPTARTMENT PATIENT SLIPPERS

Developed to be patient slippers, the adaptive troops in Vietnam sometimes used these as shower shoes. Communal shower facilities in Vietnam lead to the rapid spread of athlete's foot. Hence, few GIs ventured toward their shower, or even far from their bunk, without slipping on a pair these special shoes, which were worn through the shower......... **$15-25**

ARMY: QUARTERMASTER CORPS

FIVE-BUCKLE OVERSHOE
Soldiers likely to be exposed to water continually, such as those on river patrol craft, were issued these non-skid vinyl overshoes. They were produced in full sizes. **$20-40**

TIRE SANDALS
Since the 1940s, the people of Vietnam had been making sandals from discarded tires. With a sole made from tread, and straps made from rubber, these sandals were durable, inexpensive, and leant themselves well to the humid conditions of the country. American servicemen came to appreciate these improvised sandals for use in camp, and most servicemen returned to the states with a pair in their duffel bag. **$20-50**

DELTA COMFORT SHOE
Foot fungus was an ongoing problem for troops in Vietnam. The constant exposure to wet climate, wet socks and wet boots created a prime environment for this problem. Hence, in 1968-69, the Army procured 20,000 pairs of these canvas shoes for issue to troops in the Mekong Delta. The intention was that troops could take off their waterlogged boots and socks and put on these shoes, which gave some foot protection. **$30-50**

SPIKE-RESISTANT INSOLE
The Viet Cong were masters of the use of Punji sticks, and as mentioned earlier, the first boots issued to troops in Vietnam lacked protection from these weapons. Accordingly, Natick Labs created spike-resistant insoles. These consisted of a thin piece of white nylon glued to a piece of black rubber with thin strips of spring steel sandwiched between the two. While far from ideal, 30,000 of these were shipped to Vietnam in June 1963. . . . . **$20-30**

STANDARD INSOLE
The standard insole used by U.S. troops in Vietnam was made of gold-colored nylon. Marked "Do Not Boil," the insoles were of laminated construction stitched together. The plastic insoles were intended to provide air circulation under the feet. The label "Do Not Boil" on each insole was inspiration for the infantry joke, "Do not boil 'em, just peel 'em and eat 'em." **$5-10**

LOW-QUARTER
Black low-quarter shoes were introduced as standard issue among U.S. troops in September 1956. Troops in Vietnam were required to have black low-quarter shoes in addition to boots. **$10-30**

ARMY: Quartermaster Corps

Headgear

The primary purpose of military headgear is to protect the soldier's head from sun, rain, and of course, from wounds. A secondary function is to provide distinctive identification to friend and foe. Despite regulations, troops in the field have long tended to personalize their headgear by shaping their caps, and making other subtle changes. In Vietnam, such trends reached record highs. Straps on helmets and hats were often festooned with cigarettes, repellents and other lightweight items that needed to be kept dry and easily accessible. Helmet covers and "boonie" hats became canvases for trench art—with decorations drawn or sewn on—often to the dismay of officers.

Such customized items warrant a premium—sometimes substantial—over pristine as-issued items. However, fraudulent items are frequently encountered. Was a helmet cover decorated with a ballpoint pen in the Central Highlands four decades ago, or was it decorated in a basement in Cleveland four days ago? Provenance is critical in establishing that a premium is warranted.

This June 1970 photo of 7th Battalion, 15th Artillery personnel illustrates the diversity of headgear found in Vietnam. One soldier in the foreground wears the classic M1 steel pot with "Mitchell" pattern cover, while three others wear "boonie" hats in a variety of personal styles. National Archives photo.

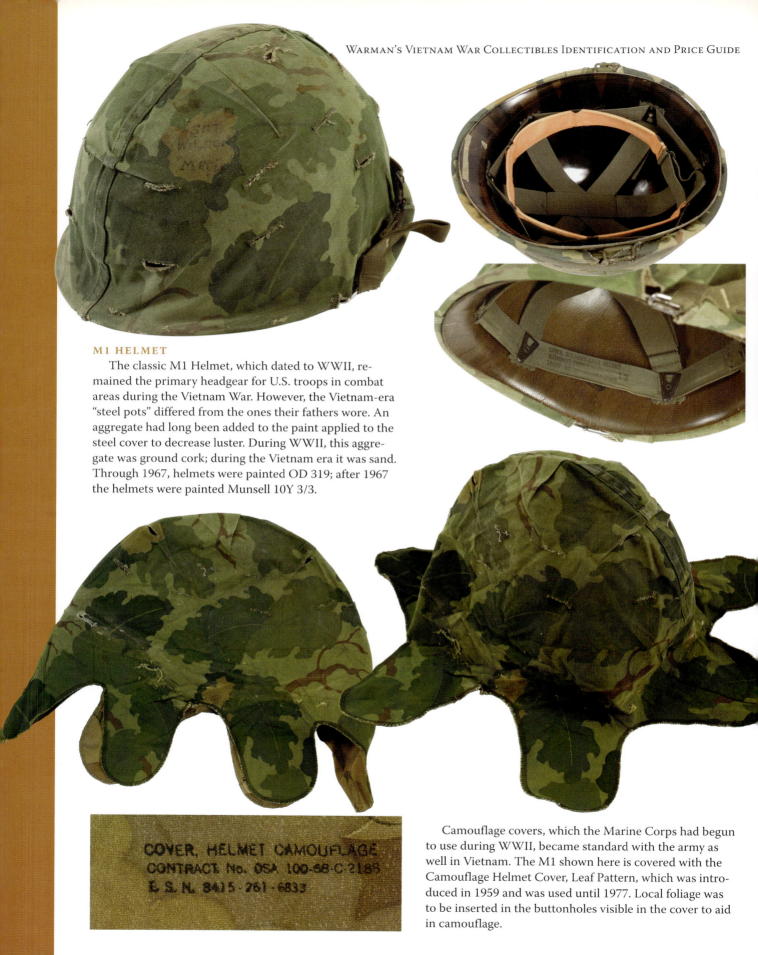

M1 HELMET

The classic M1 Helmet, which dated to WWII, remained the primary headgear for U.S. troops in combat areas during the Vietnam War. However, the Vietnam-era "steel pots" differed from the ones their fathers wore. An aggregate had long been added to the paint applied to the steel cover to decrease luster. During WWII, this aggregate was ground cork; during the Vietnam era it was sand. Through 1967, helmets were painted OD 319; after 1967 the helmets were painted Munsell 10Y 3/3.

Camouflage covers, which the Marine Corps had begun to use during WWII, became standard with the army as well in Vietnam. The M1 shown here is covered with the Camouflage Helmet Cover, Leaf Pattern, which was introduced in 1959 and was used until 1977. Local foliage was to be inserted in the buttonholes visible in the cover to aid in camouflage.

ARMY: QUARTERMASTER CORPS

Also visible in the photo is the 23-inch circumference camouflage helmet band. Though intended to secure additional concealment items, it most frequently was used to secure personal items such as insect repellent, matches, etc.

Chinstraps were issued with helmets, but were not always used.

Resin-impregnated cotton duck was used to form the M1 Helmet Liner until 1969. However, in 1962, experiments began with laminated nylon liners that offered improved protection with only a moderate increase in weight. The nylon units, known as Combat Helmet Liners, were tested in the field in Vietnam, and by 1964 the new liners were being mass produced. Production of liners with removable suspensions did not begin until late 1972, and production of liners with permanent suspensions did not end until 1974.

Helmet, with liner, chinstrap, and band. **$30-70**

COMBAT VEHICLE CREWMAN HELMET
This bullet-resistant helmet is made of ballistic nylon. The wide-open frontal area allowed the wearer to use vision and sighting systems installed in armored vehicles without having to remove the helmet. The helmet included microphone and headset. The integral cable plugged directly into the vehicle's communication system. $30-60

SPH-4 FLYER'S HELMET
The SPH-4 began replacing the earlier APH-5 flying helmet in July 1969. Both acrylic and polycarbonate visors have been used on these helmets; however, the later were not available until late in 1972. These helmets included an M87 microphone as well as headset, and were used by both helicopter and scout aircraft pilots. $75-200

RIDGEWAY CAP
In 1953, Army Chief of Staff Matthew Bunker Ridgeway directed that troops have a neat appearance, which often involved inserting cardboard stiffeners in their M1951 cotton field caps. A commercially available substitute with spring reinforcements became popular with the troops, who were willing to spend the few dollars to buy this rather than deal with stiffening their issue M1951. This commercial replacement is commonly known as the "Ridgeway Cap." This hat was used in Vietnam until July 1, 1964. . . . . $20-30

ARMY: Quartermaster Corps

The standard utility cap was found in two styles, the issue peak and a commercial cap with stiff front available through the PX.. . . . . $10-20

BASEBALL CAP

Such standard utility caps were popular with troops of all ranks in Vietnam. Initially, authorization to wear such caps was given only to aviation units and related supply units in working areas. This authority was later extended to a handful of other areas. Two styles: Issue Peak and PX mfg. with stiff front.

The hat shown here was worn by Major General Charles W. Eifler, head of First Logistical Command in Vietnam until May 1967. . . . . $10-20

TROPICAL HAT, AKA "BOONIE HAT"

Perhaps the quintessential piece of Vietnam war head gear is the Tropical Hat, sometimes referred to as a hot-weather hat or jungle hat—but known universally to GIs and collectors as the boonie hat.

Field-testing of this hat began in Vietnam during 1966, with mass production beginning the next year. However, in July 1968, General Creighton Abrams took command of MACV, and he strongly disliked the boonie hat, largely because it lent itself to individualization and because of its non-rigid shape. By late 1971, Abrams and his staff had, for all intents and purposes, eliminated the boonie hat. The boonie hat was most commonly found in olive drab $20-30

CAMOUFLAGED TROPICAL HAT

A limited number of the boonie hats were produced with the ERDL camouflage pattern. These hats were not widely used in Vietnam, in part because they were not produced in this pattern until immediately before Abram's virtual ban on this style of cover...................... $40-60

ARMY: Quartermaster Corps

BUSH HAT
Vietnamese-made "bush" hats were popular with advisors from 1962-66. The advent of the tropical "boonie" hat contributed to the demise of the bush hat, which typically had only local authorization. The example shown here has the tiger-stripe camouflage pattern. **$75-125**

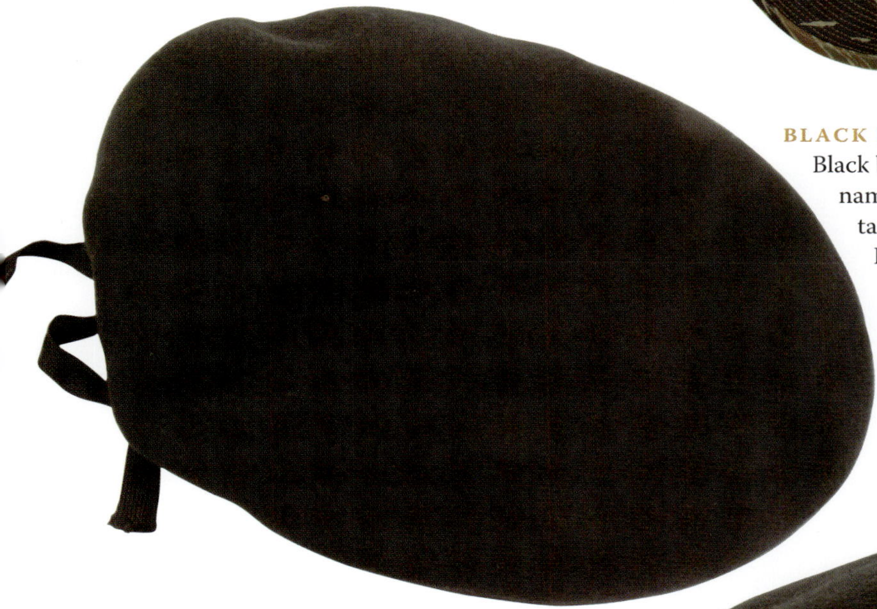

BLACK BERET
Black berets were worn by a host of units in Vietnam. Among these were advisors to ARVN tank and mechanized units, National Police Force, Mobile Advisory Teams, as well as U.S. scout dog and combat tracker teams and certain Ranger units. **$40-60**

GREEN BERET
Made famous by the Army Special Forces, the Rifle Green Army shade 297 wool beret is arguably the most famous piece of headgear to come out of the war. It is also the only beret officially approved for wear by men in the Army during the Vietnam War. **$250-350**

ARMY

Despite the highly mechanized nature of the Vietnam War, the primary means of transporting a soldier's gear remained his back. These 2nd Battalion, 27th Infantry, 25th Infantry Division soldiers operating in the Mekong Delta in August 1970 exhibit the typical burden of the GI. National Archives photo.

Individual Equipment

The soldier in the field was prepared for many circumstances. Fighting, subsistence, shelter from the weather, first aid and sleeping were among the needs of each soldier. To carry all of this gear—which is described elsewhere in this volume—the military developed a variety of load-carrying equipment for the individual solder. Most GIs in Vietnam were issued an assortment of the gear described in the following section. To this was added additional equipment as needed for particular tasks. The items listed in this portion of the book distinguish soldiers operating in the field from those working at permanent installations.

ARMY: QUARTERMASTER CORPS

The 2-1/4-inch wide cotton web belt M1956 is dyed OD 7. The first pattern belt (made prior to 1967) had a ball-hook buckle. The FSN of the belt is 8465-577-4925. ....$20-30

From 1967 on, the M1956 Individual Equipment Belt was equipped with the Davis T-slot connector.
.... $15-25

The M1956 belt is shown here with a typical array of field gear.

Poncho, Coated Nylon Twill, FSN 8405-290-0550, included a permanently attached hood and waist drawstrings. Troops in Vietnam found many uses for ponchos beyond basic rainwear. This particular style poncho was not 100-percent satisfactory, and during the late 1960s, testing had begun on a lighter poncho......... **$50-75**

ARMY: QUARTERMASTER CORPS

Clean drinking water has always been critical for troops in the field. At the outset of the U.S. involvement in Vietnam, the classic aluminum M1910 Canteen with plastic cap was standard issue. **$15-30**

The Arctic Canteen, FSN 8465-753-6489, and cover, FSN 8465-753-6490, was widely used by Special Forces in the early part of the Vietnam War. **$10-20**

Two-quart collapsible canteen (film bladder) cover, FSN 8465-889-3769. Made by International Latex Corp., these were based on their WWII design. . . **$10-15**

In 1962 this new olive drag plastic canteen began to replace the M1910 canteen. The new one-quart canteen had a pastic screw cap which was retained by a plastic strap. Look on the bottom to verify the date of these FSN 8465-889-3744 canteens.. . . . . **$5-10**

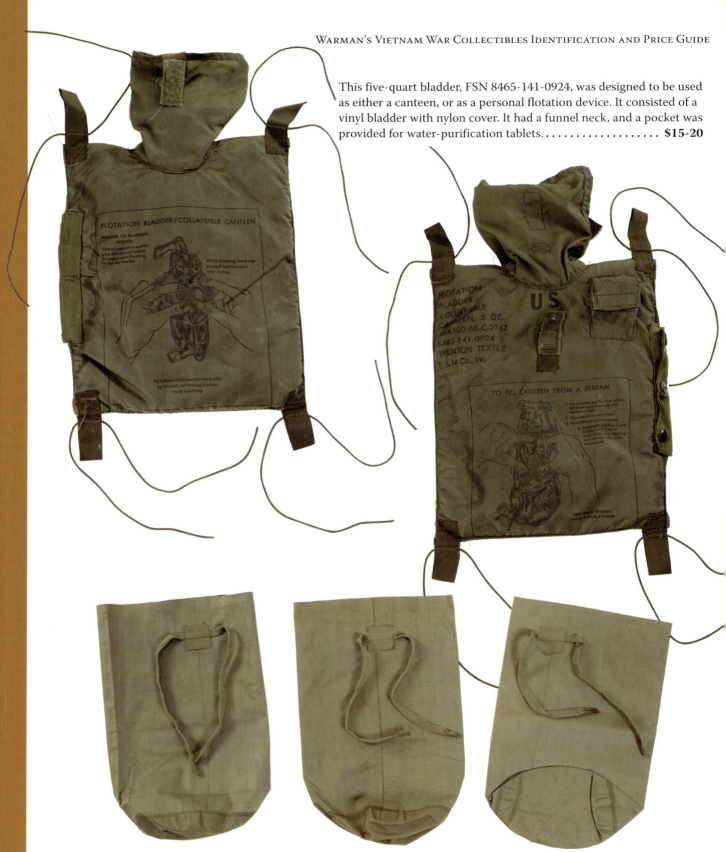

This five-quart bladder, FSN 8465-141-0924, was designed to be used as either a canteen, or as a personal flotation device. It consisted of a vinyl bladder with nylon cover. It had a funnel neck, and a pocket was provided for water-purification tablets. **$15-20**

These are the three waterproof bags that were issued with the early style Tropical Rucksack. They are a light green cotton cloth with a rubberized treatment inside. They are intended to be inserted into each of the three external pockets on the rucksack. A larger one was supposed to be available for the pack's main compartment. A later style bag was made of lighter weight nylon material. The later issues were a dark OD color that matched the rucksack. Usually missing from collector packs.

ARMY: Quartermaster Corps

Bag, Waterproof, Clothing FSN 8465-261-6909. This was an OG 106 bag made to mil spec MIL-B-3108. Any type of water-resistant bag was desirable in Vietnam. **$2-10**

Troops in the northern parts of Vietnam were issued the traditional "U.S." marked OG118 wool blanket. The FSN was 7210-715-7985, and it was made to spec MIL-B-844. . . . . **$10-20**

The first pattern M1956 suspenders were part of the basic issue item as U.S. troops arrived in Vietnam. Hooks were on the front and rear straps. The front hooks included loops for attaching the sleeping-gear carrier. A loop was also at the bottom edge of each shoulder pad so an ammunition case could be connected. Three sizes were issued: Regular, Long and X-Long. $15-20

n 1961, the 2nd pattern M1956 suspenders began to be issued. Snap hooks were used on the rear straps, while the front hooks were now made from flat rather than rounded steel stock. Three sizes were issued: Regular, Long and X-Long.. . . . . $15-20

The M1956 Combat Field Pack "Butt Pack" was the typical field pack used when U.S. forces were first deployed to Vietnam. The pack, which was made of OD7 cotton duck, had a row of eyelets on its flap. These were to be used to suspend a variety of gear. As issued, the pack could be attached to a pistol belt or, through the use of adapter straps, it could be worn higher up. The FSN for the M1956 Combat Field Pack was 8465-577-4921. . . . . $20-30

ARMY: QUARTERMASTER CORPS

Soldiers who wanted to carry the butt pack on their back, rather than suspending it from their belt, used these M1956 cotton field pack adapter straps. Frequently referred to as Butt Pack Adapter Straps, they were assigned FSN 8465-782-2170. . . . . $10-15

The M1961 Combat Field Pack "Butt Pack" was an improved model of the M1956. Chief among the modifications was a waterproof throat lining for the storage compartment. The M1961 Field Pack, canvas, was assigned FSN 8465-823-7622, and was made according to specification MIL-F-40165. . . . . $15-25

The Sling, Universal, Individual Load Carrying, FSN 8465-753-3257, was used to allow soldiers to carry a wide variety of gear in the field. Though all were made to specification MIL-S-43013, a variety of stitching methods were used.
....$5-10

ARMY: Quartermaster Corps

Part of the M1956 Load Carrying Equipment was this Strap Assembly, Carrier, Sleeping Bag. Assigned FSN 8465-647-0851, these straps were created to support a sleeping bag from the M1956 Suspenders. Because many troops in Vietnam did not use the issue sleeping bag, these straps were used for a variety of improvised purposes.... **$15-15**

The Tropical Rucksack, FSN 8465-935-6673, replaced the Lightweight Rucksack with the riveted frame. These were issued late, probably in 1971 or after. The owner of this one has included extra items worn attached to the outside of the pack, typical of those worn in the field. Two extra one-quart water canteens fastened with snap links or "carabiners," the latest lightweight folding handle entrenching tool in nylon carrier, and a machete stowed in the loop behind one of the external pockets on the pack. **$125-165**

The Rucksack, Nylon Duck, FSN 8465-782-3248, was a lightweight piece of load-carrying equipment designed to be attached to a tubular frame, as seen here. $200-250

The M79 grenade vest could carry 24 rounds for the M79 grenade launcher, and had mesh shoulders and back for ventilation. $10-20

ARMY: Quartermaster Corps

Body Armor

M1952A FLAK JACKET

Known officially as "Armor, Body, Fragmentation, Protective, Upper Torso, M-1952A," this Korean War-vintage bit of body armor soldiered on for the duration of the Vietnam War, despite newer designs being introduced. The M1952A weighed 8 1/2 pounds, and like all the other "flak jackets" used during the Vietnam War, were not designed as "bullet-proof" vests, but rather to protect the wearer from shell and grenade fragments. They were designed to be worn over the shirt but under the jacket. The jacket had nylon protection, epaulets and a zip-front closure, and was produced according to specification MIL-A-12370.................................. **$125-225**

T66-1 LIGHTWEIGHT BODY ARMOR
This 4-pound, 8-ounce vest was developed specifically to provide troops serving in the hot tropic environment with a more wearable form of body protection. The vest was demonstrated in February and March of 1966, and 400 were procured for extended field test during late 1966 and early 1967. This vest is arguably the scarcest piece of body armor used in Vietnam. **$300-400**

M69 FLAK VEST W/O STIFFENERS
In 1965 an improved flak jacket was introduced. Similar to the M1952A, the new jacket lacked epaulets, but had a 3/4-inch collar. This collar was intended to protect the wearer's neck, but users complained that in interfered with the M1 helmet. The jacket was made of OG-106 nylon, and the protection was from 12 plies of ballistic nylon. Elastic draw cords were on each side and grenade hangers over both cargo pockets. This jacket is sometimes referred to as the "823-series" by collectors due to the center digits of the Federal Stock Number. It was constructed according to military specifications MIL-B-12370. . . . . **$125-225**

M69 FLAK VEST W/STIFFENERS
In 1968, the specification for the vest, MIL-B-12370, was changed. Now polyethylene stiffeners were located in the fifth layer of the ballistic nylon. Previously, the ballistic nylon had a tendency to become bunched up, greatly reducing protection. This vest, known to some collectors as the "122-series", was at first closed with a zipper. **$125-225**

M69 FLAK VEST W/STIFFENERS VELCRO FASTENER
Shortly after the introduction of the stiffeners, MIL-B-12370 was changed again, resulting in yet another version of the M69. At this time the zipper closure was replaced with a Velcro fastener. Velcro also replaced the snaps previously used for pocket flap closures. Interestingly, in addition to the four standard sizes provided for American troops, three smaller sizes were made for use by Vietnamese soldiers. The body of the vest continued to be made from OG-106 nylon with elastic side laces. These vests were also "122-series" items. **$125-225**

ARMY: Quartermaster Corps

Company D, 2nd Battalion, 3rd Infantry, 199th Light Infantry Brigade, moves out from Long Binh, Vietnam, in October 1969. Notice the lightweight pack frame being used to transport the radio. National Archives photo.

Field Gear

A wide variety of items are needed to keep an army operational in the field. While some of these items are reusable, such as field desks and hammocks, other items are consumable, such as weapons. Collectors today seek such items, particularly if they want to create an impression of "life in the field" for a military unit, rather than an inspection-ready, footlocker-type display.

The Field Desk was typically used by the company clerk. These portable units fold into a simple box, with the two furnished stools stored under the lid/desktop. Made of plywood, the desk included several drawers...... **$75-175**

Often used on heavier weapons, such as the M60 and M2 machine guns, was this Lubricant, Weapons, Semi-fluid, High Load Carrying, known as LSAT. It came in 8-ounce and 16-ounce tubes. Shown here is the 8-ounce tube, FSN 9150-949-0323. ....**$3-5**

ARMY: QUARTERMASTER CORPS

PL-S was the designation given to general-purpose lubricating oil, which often came in this small 4-ounce can. It is a water-displacing, preservative lubricating oil often used on small arms and automatic weapons.... $2-4

Rifle Bore Cleaner was also furnished in 6-ounce steel cans, some of it dating back as far as WWII. These were more often found in camp than in the field. $3-5

General-purpose Lubricating Oil was also packaged in one-quart steel cans. This type of package was commonly found in arms rooms and on vehicles with mounted automatic weapons.
...............$3-5

LSA was the designation given to this silicone-based Weapons Oil Medium. Two-ounce bottles like these were widely carried in the field. Various vendors supplied this product, with slight variations in the markings on the refillable bottles. $2-4

These 2-ounce plastic bottles of Rifle Bore Cleaner were found in the gear of virtually every armed GI in Vietnam............$2-4

One-pound cans of this dark-green rifle grease were used when placing weapons in long-term storage. The heavy grease prevented rust and corrosion. This large can was also used for refilling the small tubs of this grease found in most cleaning kits, and in the stock of the M14......$5-10

Because of the hot, wet climate in Vietnam, ammunition for the M16 was sometimes packed in disposable plastic bags. At some point it was decided that these bags, typically discarded wherever they were opened, should be imprinted with a "Chieu Hoi" (Open Arms) message reading, *"Returning Chieu Hoi will help you to again see your parents and family in a peaceful and democratic South Vietnam."* Chieu Hoi was a massive PSYOP campaign aimed at persuading Viet Cong guerrillas to change allegiances. **$10-15**

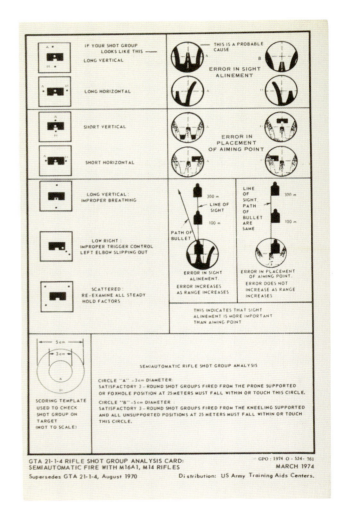

This is a Graphical Training Aid or GTA 21-1-4. Printed on heavy card stock, the 4-inch by 6-inch instructions illustrated the correct rifle sight picture for accurate fire with the M14 and M16. The illustrations show the cause and effect of incorrect sight alignment on the target. **$4-8**

The M15 sighting device was a training aid first developed during WWII. Through the years various versions were developed for use with the M1 Garand, the M14 and the M16 (shown here). It was used to instruct students on proper placement of the target with respect to the rear sights on the weapon. **$4-8**

ARMY: Quartermaster Corps

Sandbags have been an element of fortifications for decades. The sandbags used by U.S. forces during the later part of the Vietnam War were made of woven olive-drab nylon and came with black drawstring closures.......$2-3

Sandbag revetments protect various areas of Landing Zone Bronco in Cambodia. Millions of sandbags were used for such purposes during the war. When new, the bags were olive drab, but they quickly faded in the tropical sun. National Archives photo.

As has been the case for GIs since the American Civil War, each soldier going into the field carried a shelter half, along with five stakes and a three-piece wooden pole. Two halves, with their associated stakes and poles, formed a two-man pup tent.

Each of the three-piece tent poles was dated. At the top is a 1957-dated pole, and at the bottom a 1961-dated pole. On one end of each wooden pole was a metal tip, and on the other end a metal ferrule, allowing the pole sections to be joined. $15-20

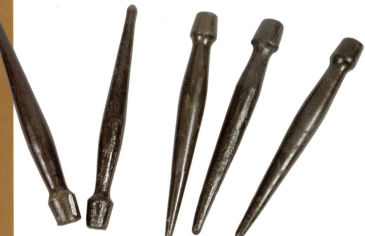

Early in the Vietnam War, some of these WWII-era wooden stakes were used. However, these were quickly replaced with newer metal stakes. In either event, the shelter half was rarely used as intended in Vietnam. $1-2

Aluminum tent stakes were by far more common in Vietnam, although the shelter half more frequently served as a ground cloth than as a tent in country. $1-2

ARMY: QUARTERMASTER CORPS

Hammocks were an oft-used field bedding. The M-1965 hammock was waterproof, and fairly rugged, and reasonably popular with the troops. $100-125

The clutter on the back of the M551 Sheridan tank that these 25th Infantry Division soldiers are riding on gives an idea of the amount of equipment, both authorized and unauthorized, that American soldiers carried onto the battlefield. National Archives photo.

Claymore antipersonnel mines came in this canvas satchel. To use the mine, it was removed from the bag, and many soldiers found these bags excellent for carry personal items. Instructions for setting up the mine were sewn into the inside of the bag. **$15-25**

This collapsible cotton shower pail included a metal showerhead in its bottom. It was used in an effort to provide troops with a means of showering in the field. The pail held 5 gallons of water. **$35-55**

ARMY: Quartermaster Corps

Soldiers were issued individually packed 4-ounce cakes of soap, FSN 8520-129-0803. As one would expect for such a fragile, easily degraded and utilitarian item, few survive today. $2-4

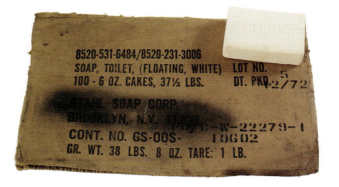

Cakes of soap were also packaged in bulk, in cases of 100. These 6-ounce cakes were commonly found in permanent posts. The collector value is primarily in the packaging. $2-4/bar

The Individual Survival Kit - Type IV was originally developed for use by aircrews. However, in Vietnam it became popular with the famed "tunnel rats." The kit included a burning lens and a sharpening stone, but the centerpiece was the survival ax with its canvas carrying case. The FSN for the survival kit was 8465-973-4807. . . . . $125-175

WARMAN'S VIETNAM WAR COLLECTIBLES IDENTIFICATION AND PRICE GUIDE

The Kit, Survival, Individual, Operational Packet contained the basics for survival until rescue, including a flare gun, bandages, water purification tablets, signal mirror, saw, bullion cubes and numerous other items. It was packed in a plastic box, within an olive-drab nylon waterproof bag. . . $30-60

Survival Kit, Individual contained matches, fishing hooks and line, water purification tablets, heavy aluminum foil and an assortment of bandages, items useful to keeping a man alive in adverse conditions. $30-60

ARMY: Quartermaster Corps

The confidential document case was to be used to secure eyes-only documents. When full, this case was to be kept locked and under supervision. **$75-125**

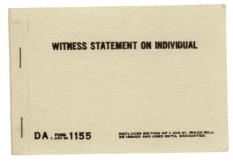

A single copy of DA Form 1155, Witness Statement on Individual, was to be carried by each solider. Squad leaders and platoon sergeants were encouraged to carry a booklet of 1155s. This form was used to report deaths where the remains were not recovered, or individuals who were missing, captured, interned or detained. **$5-10**

A single copy of DA Form 1156, Casualty Feeder Report, was to be carried by each solider. Squad leaders and platoon sergeants were encouraged to carry a booklet of 1156s. This form was used to report all friendly casualties witnessed or encountered, to include American civilians, soldiers from other units or services, and allied soldiers. **$5-10**

Vehicular or equipment document record pouch, made of heavy-duty, mildew-resistant olive-drab canvas. Any piece of mechanical equipment that had an internal-combustion engine had a maintenance record book stored on the machine or vehicle, and this bag was designed to contain these documents, as well as the operation manual. It was secured with metal clips at the back. **$10-15**

Photographed in Cambodia in 1970, members of Company A, 1st Battalion, 5th Infantry, 1st Cavalry Division (Airmobile) begin a brief mission. Each soldier has a bandoleer of ammunition, smoke grenades, canteens and a host of other equipment. National Archives photo.

Accoutrements

Soldiers operating in the field carry with them an array of items that are needed not just for their mission, but also for their survival. The specifics of what was carried varied depending upon the mission and its duration. Other gear, such as duffel bags, was used primarily to get the GI to his "home away from home". These include canteens, first-aid kits, compasses, shelter and a host of other items – all of which are collectible today.

ARMY: Quartermaster Corps

The Case, Ammunition, Shotgun, FSN 8465-261-8944 is made of cotton duck and holds 12 shotgun shells. Two belt loops on the back were used to secure the case to the belt. Shotguns were most commonly used in Vietnam for security work. $20-30

Soldiers operating in the field felt that the waterproof bag, rucksack liner or a similar item was essential. Not only swamp-like conditions, but high humidity and frequent rainfall, made keeping gear dry difficult. $8-12

The Bag, Duffel, was essentially the soldier's suitcase. Two styles were used, above is the later style with shoulder harness and a pocket for orders. Below the late bag is an early bag, distinguished by its single shoulder strap. The early bag was in use from WWII into the 1960s. Both styles are frequently found today with the GI's name written on it
.... **$10-20**

Barracks Bag or "Laundry bag." These were made from a lightweight cotton poplin material, and in Vietnam were different from the previous heavy cotton khaki or OD bags of WWII and Korean vintage; same material as the tropical uniforms. **$10-20**

ARMY: Quartermaster Corps

The traditional GI canteen was carried in this pouch, which served many purposes beyond merely a means of transport. The canteen pouch hid the metal of the canteen, insulated the canteen and reduced noise. $5-10

This PFC returning from a 1966 night patrol is carrying the typical burden of a soldier in such duty. The load-carrying equipment typically being used at this time was developed shortly after the Korean War, and was found to be excessively heavy and subject to degradation not only from the humidity in Vietnam, but from the GI's perspiration. National Archives photo.

Part of the M1956 load-carrying equipment, the Universal Ammunition pouch (FSN 8465-647-0852) would hold short magazines for the M14 or M16 rifle. A variety of stencil markings were used through the Vietnam era on these pouches. The second-pattern M1956 Universal Small Arms Ammunition Pouch was not as rigid as the first pattern, but retained the 8465-647-0852 FSN............................ **$10-12**

Shorter than the Universal Ammunition pouch, the M1956 20rd M16A1 Magazine Pouch (FSN 8465-935-4871) was designed to hold four 20-round clips for the M16................................... **$15-20**

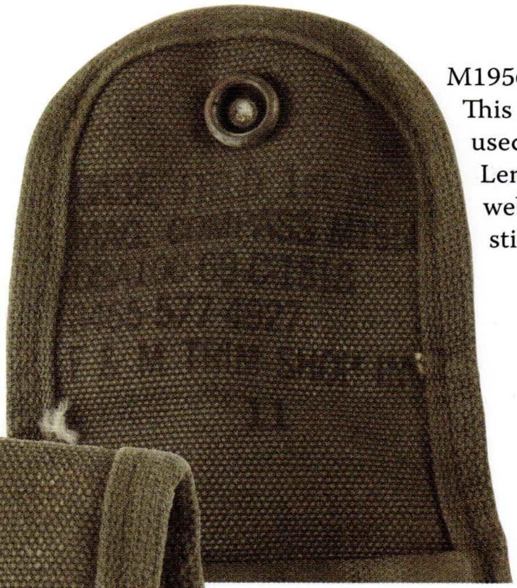

ARMY: QUARTERMASTER CORPS

M1956 First Aid/Compass Case, first pattern. This canvas pouch, FSN 8465-577-4927, was used to carry either first-aid dressing or a Lensatic compass. It was part of the M1956 web gear, and the first pattern did not have stitched edging or drain holes.

Unlike the first version, the second-pattern M1956 First Aid/Compass Case, FSN 8465-577-4927, incorporated drain holes and stitched edging. A single slide keeper was provided for attaching to belt or suspenders. **$15-20**

111

Map and compass reading were necessary survival skills as well as requirements for successful co-ordination of infantry, artillery, armored and air operations. Accordingly, all troops were trained in the use of compasses and maps, although only officers and NCOs were normally issued compasses.

The standard-issue compass during the Vietnam era was this Lensatic Compass, typified by this 1966-dated example. During the course of the war, the compass was manufactured by various contractors, including Jay Bee Corp, Stocker and Yale, and Superior Magneto. The compass could be folded compactly for carrying. Beware of low-quality, non-issue copies of this compass.

The compass is shown here with the early Olive Drab M1942 first-aid pouch, which has the M1910 wire hanger attachment. Later WWII examples of this style canvas pouch are dual purpose, marked on the back for first-aid packet or for the Lensatic compass. This case was replaced by the M1956 Canvas pouch. This documented example was carried in Vietnam combat in 1968 by a company commander of the 101st Airborne Division.......... **$50-75**

A Lensatic Compass is shown here with the dual-purpose canvas M-1956 Case, First Aid Packet or Lensatic Compass. The case has the single ALICE or sliding-clip attachment system on the reverse side and was frequently attached to the Field Pack Suspenders. As the markings indicate, it could be used to carry either the compass or first-aid packet. It is shown here open for use, and partially open with its markings exposed................. **$50-75**

ARMY: QUARTERMASTER CORPS

The Graphic Training Aid (GTA) 5-15 was developed during WWII to teach troops the basic use of military map coordinates and compass orientation. Printed and assembled on heavy card stock, pocket-sized, it includes a simple clear plastic replica of a Lensatic compass that can be rotated on a brass grommet. **$10-15**

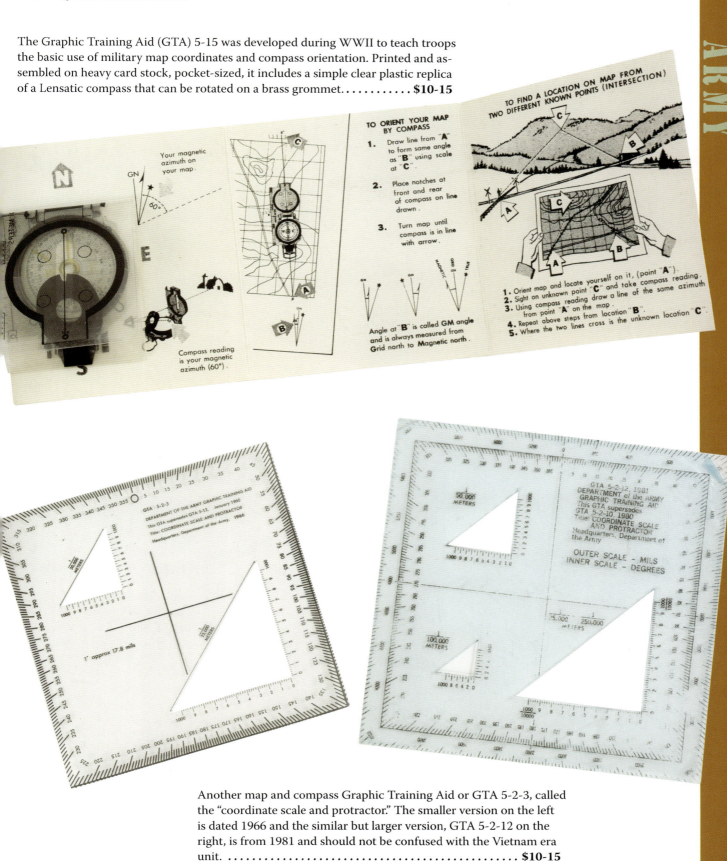

Another map and compass Graphic Training Aid or GTA 5-2-3, called the "coordinate scale and protractor." The smaller version on the left is dated 1966 and the similar but larger version, GTA 5-2-12 on the right, is from 1981 and should not be confused with the Vietnam era unit. **$10-15**

Although Vietnam is traditionally thought of as a steamy tropic, at night in the highlands temperatures could get uncomfortably cold. Troops were issued this feather-filled M-1945 sleeping bag. This had been the army's standard sleeping bag since WWII, so the date on the tag is important to verify Vietnam-era manufacture. $20-40

This "carrying strap assembly" was part of the M1956 web gear. It was designed to support the sleeping bag.

This carrying bag (FSN 8465-261-4989) was provided to store and transport a sleeping bag. In Vietnam it was used for a range of other purposes as well. $15-20

ARMY: Quartermaster Corps

As its name implies, the M1967 Sleeping Gear Carrier, FSN 8465-935-6813, was designed to transport a sleeping bag. Depending upon the part of Vietnam in which they were operating, troops who did not need a sleeping bag used the OG-106 water-repellent 7-1/4-ounce nylon duck bag to transport other gear they wished to keep dry. . . . **$15-20**

This shelf was used with pack frames to carry radios, water cans and other firm, awkward pieces of gear. **$20-25**

Accoutrements are generally thought of with respect to infantry - but are actually related to all troops. Vehicle crewman tended to festoon their vehicles not only with their issued gear, but extras they were able to scavenge as well. Such is the case with this M42A1 Duster crew, here being photographed by Signal Corps photographer in the Dak To province during July 1967.

This OG106 Bag, Waterproof, Clothing, FSN 8465-261-6909, was occasionally used in conjunction with a duffel bag to provide waterproof protection for uniforms and gear. $10-15

Scouts pause to refill their canteens from a stream north of An Khe. The soldier's M16 is within arms reach as he fills two bladder canteens, and one hard plastic one in January 1969. Looking through the pages of this volume we can see that troops were burdened with a lot of gear, but few items were as important as the canteen.

ARMY: Quartermaster Corps

The olive drab cotton duck M1938 Map Case had two large pockets for maps plus several slots for writing instruments. It was worn suspended by a detachable shoulder strap......$40-70

The M1951 combination tool was the entrenching tool carried by GIs through much of the war. It had a wooden handle, and two heavy steel blades – a pick and a shovel. These blades could be set at various angles. It was housed in a canvas carrier. Be sure and look for the U.S. and manufacturer markings on these tools.
.... $20-40

The lightweight entrenching tool was developed in 1967. Two slightly different versions were produced, and almost one million of them were shipped to Vietnam. While soldiers appreciated the weight savings and improved carrier, these new aluminum tools were not as rugged as the old ones – nor did they make good improvised weapons. Be sure to look for the U.S. and manufacturer markings on these tools. $20-40

ARMY: Quartermaster Corps

U.S. troops wore a wide variety of uniforms during the Vietnam War. In the foreground of this 1970 photo can just be seen a soldier clad in the famous "Tiger Stripe" uniform, while the other two GIs are wearing OG-107 fatigues. National Archives photo.

In this August 1970 photo, the bulk of these 2nd Battalion, 27th Infantry, 25th Infantry Division troops preparing for a long-range reconnaissance patrol are wearing the ERDL camouflage uniform, while a single soldier in the left foreground wears a OG-107 uniform. National Archives photo.

U.S. Army Uniforms

The values for clothing items listed below assume new or used but excellent serviceable condition. Clothing, especially shirts and jackets, with a provenance of actual use in Vietnam can be expected to bring a premium. Also, larger sizes tend to be valued more than smaller sizes.

Undergarments

Like their T-shirts, the underwear of troops in Vietnam began as white, from the FSN 8420-682-6593 series, but quickly changed to Olive Green. The olive green 109 drawers were from the FSN 8420-782-6405 series. **$15-20**

In the early stages of the war, white T-shirts of the FSN 8420-543-6643 series were issued. However troops quickly dyed those dark colors. Ultimately, troops in Vietnam were issued five of these OG 109 T-shirts, which were of the FSN 8420-782-6707 series. **$15-20**

The socks issued to GI's in Vietnam were wool with a cushioned sole. They were of a stretch type, and dyed OG 408. They were from the FSN 8440-782-2171 series. It was not uncommon for soldiers to use extra socks as a means to carry ration cans.
. . . .**$5-10**

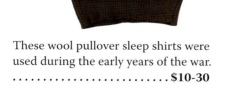

While armchair generals think of Vietnam solely as a hot place, this was not always true. Nights, particularly in the central highlands, were quite cold. Hence, troops were issued sleep shirts to be worn at night.

These wool pullover sleep shirts were used during the early years of the war.
. . . . **$10-30**

Later in the war, the Shirt, Sleeping, Heat Retentive and Moisture Resistant made of nylon/triacetate began to be used. These pullover OG 106 shirts were part of the 8415-890-2100 series. **$10-40**

ARMY: Quartermaster Corps

Shirts/Jackets

Maybe 1952-pattern utility jacket

This is what is commonly referred to as a second-pattern Jungle Fatigue Coat. It differed from the first-pattern jacket by having hidden rather than exposed buttons, and did not have a gas flap. The official nomenclature is Jungle Fatigue Coat, Man's, Combat, Tropical DSA100-1387. . . . . **$30-60**

The third pattern of the Jungle Fatigue Coat was made of wind-resistant cotton poplin dyed OG-107. Unlike its predecessors, it did not have shoulder tabs. These were introduced in 1967 and were from the 8405-935-4702 series. **$30-60**

WARMAN'S VIETNAM WAR COLLECTIBLES IDENTIFICATION AND PRICE GUIDE

COAT, BUSH, HOT-WET, T-54-4, EXPERIMENTAL
Lightweight green coat with four flapped pockets on front. Dark brown plastic buttons. Cotton belt with gold gilt sliding buckle. Experimental hot-weather bush jacket that was not adopted.
. . . . **Too rarely traded to establish accurate value.**

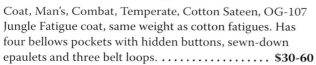

Coat, Man's, Combat, Temperate, Cotton Sateen, OG-107 Jungle Fatigue coat, same weight as cotton fatigues. Has four bellows pockets with hidden buttons, sewn-down epaulets and three belt loops. **$30-60**

Shirt, man's cotton, OG-107, special warfare. Epaulets added in the field. **$15-25**

ARMY: Quartermaster Corps

This long-sleeve, OG-107 single-breasted jungle jacket, with four cargo pockets with flaps and buttons on each side at chest and one on each side at waist, was known as Coat, Man's, Cotton, Water-Resistant, Poplin. The jacket, part of series FSN 8405-082-5569, fastens in front with five concealed buttons. $30-60

This Coat, Man's, Combat, Tropical, dyed OG-107 was made of lightweight wind-resistant, rip-stop cotton poplin. The single-breasted garment with concealed buttons was designed to be worn with the tail outside of trousers. The cargo pockets featured flaps and double buttons. . . $30-60

Coat, Man's, Combat, Tropical, Camouflage, Lightweight wind-resistant cotton poplin. Single-breasted. The ERDL (Engineer Research and Development Laboratory) camo-pattern jacket was designed to be worn with the tail outside of trousers. It had concealed buttons, cargo pockets with flaps and double buttons. Several variations of this pattern, with different colors dominant in each variation. $300-450

123

Shirt, Jungle, Camouflage. This dark- and light-green and black shirt (left) was made in Vietnam. It has a 2-inch lay-down-type collar and two patch pockets with flaps and buttons on each side of the chest. Four small gray plastic buttons close the shirt.
.... $250-350

In 1963, the Counter Insurgency Support Office (CISO) was established on Okinawa. This office supplied Special Forces in Vietnam, often with untraceable gear. This jacket (right), sometimes referred to as Leopard Spot Pattern, is an example of the CISO products. The Vietnamese called this pattern Beo-Gam.
.... $250-350

Authentic tiger-stripe pattern uniform items, like this jacket (left), are among the most desirable Vietnam-era collectibles. Around 20 different patterns have been identified, and as with many items from this era, there are a number of reproductions on the market, which typically trade for about 10 percent of the value of an authentic item. An excellent reference on these uniforms is Tiger Patterns by Richard Johnson. $500-2,500

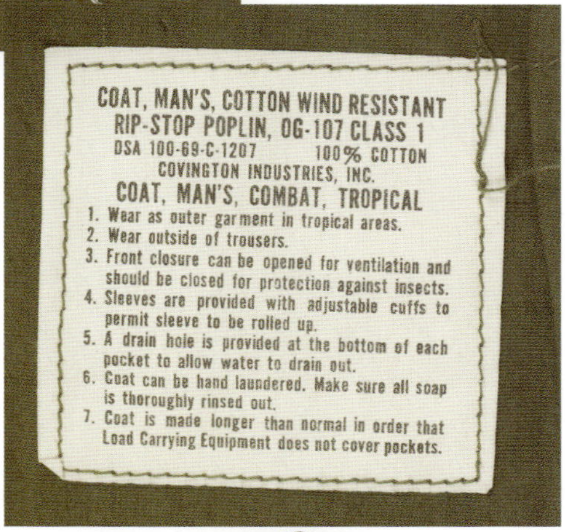

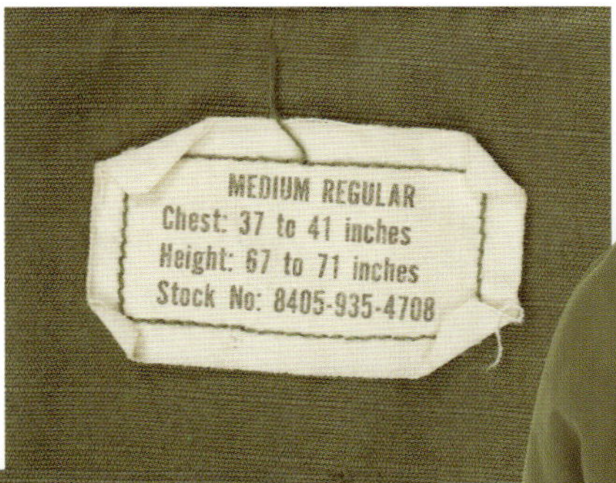

ARMY: QUARTERMASTER CORPS

Rip-stop fabric superceded the non-rip-stop material in regular OG-107 coats, beginning with the 8405-935-4708 series, which were made to specification MIL-T-43217.
....$8-20

TROUSERS

These are the first-pattern Trousers, Field. The exposed buttons on these thick, water-repellent cotton pants distinguish them from later generations. The trousers feature a button fly and the front of the waistline continues as belt fastening to metal buckle. Hip and front pockets, and as well as a cargo pocket on left leg, are characteristics of these trousers. **$50-100**

Trousers, Men's, Combat, Tropical, Rip-Stop. Lightweight cotton poplin, zipper fly, hidden-type pockets at waist, large cargo pockets on each leg with flaps and double buttons, drawstrings at the bottom of each leg. **$25-50**

These olive cotton rip-stop trousers are considered the fifth pattern, and are among the most commonly available on the market today. . . **$40-60**

Trousers, Men's, Combat, Tropical, Camouflage, lightweight rip-stop cotton poplin with adjustable waist size, hidden pockets on each side of waist, large cargo pockets on each leg with flaps and double buttons, drawstrings at the bottom of each leg. Part of 8415-945-9218 series. **$100-150**

ARMY: Quartermaster Corps

Trousers, Cotton, Sateen, Aggressor, T-60-2, OG-107. Two slash-front and two rear-button patch pockets, button-type fly. During the Cold War and through the close of the Vietnam War, U.S. troops trained against aggressor forces. Though by the end of the Vietnam War the aggressor troops were outfitted with Soviet-style uniforms, early on the uniforms were purely fictitious. . . . . **Too rarely traded to establish accurate pricing.**

Trousers, Men's, Combat, Tropical were made in Vietnam. They have a button fly and hidden pockets. On the knees were patch-type pockets with flaps and double buttons. $200-300

These green, black, brown, and white jungle camouflage trousers were privately purchased in Japan in 1965. This type uniform is commonly called "The Tiger Suit" and was issued to U.S. Special Forces and civilian irregulars. $100-150

ARMY

127

These thin lightweight cotton camouflage jungle trousers were supplied to Special Forces in Vietnam by the Counter Insurgency Support Office. This camouflage pattern is usually referred to as the Leopard Spot, or Beo-Gam, pattern. The trousers have a button fly, two patch pockets on front, and two patch pockets on back. $100-150

The black, dark- and light-green tiger-stripe pattern of these Trousers, Jungle, Camouflage is commonly called the John Wayne Dense pattern because it was worn by the actor in the movie The Green Berets. The trousers are made from thin lightweight cotton, have a button fly, two patch pockets on front and two patch pockets on back. $100-150

Collectors have identified 20-odd different tiger-stripe camouflage patterns. These trousers, Jungle, Camouflage, exhibit one of the black, green and brown patterns worn in Vietnam during 1965-66. They are made of thin lightweight cotton, have a zipper fly, and five patch pockets. $100-150

ARMY: QUARTERMASTER CORPS

Made to specification MIL-T-838, the Trousers, Utility, Cotton Sateen, OG-107, were made from non-rip-stop fabric. The trousers had two patch pockets and two hip pockets. The pocket flaps were straight cut. These trousers were part of the 8405-082-6610 series. **$20-40**

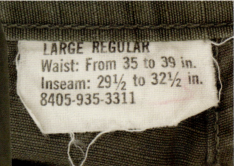

Rip-stop OG-107 fabric superceded the non-rip-stop material in regular trousers, beginning with the 8405-935-3310 series, which were made to specification MIL-T-43217. . . . . **$10-20**

Rations and Subsistence Items

Proper nutrition is critical for an effective fighting force—and palatable food is critical for good morale. Hence, in Vietnam, the Quartermaster Corps went to lengths to provide hot meals as often as possible. Nevertheless, on many occasions, troops in the field had to survive on individual rations. Here members of Battery C, 1st Battalion, 83rd Artillery, 5th Artillery Group pass through a chow line in April 1968.

The Army's Quartermaster Corps has been responsible for feeding the troops since 1775. The period immediately prior to and during WWII was marked by great advances in ration development. Most of the food items consumed during the Vietnam War were refinements of the WWII-era ration. The majority of food prepared during the Vietnam was the **Standard B ration**. These were large bulk rations designed for mass feedings in mess halls, and today are of little interest to collectors.

The **small detachment ration, 5 man**, was engineered for use by small groups such as gun and tank crews. Each of the five different menus were intended to be eaten hot, but due to the packaging this ration was not suitable for issue to individuals. That is, this could not reasonably be used to feed one man for five days. These rations have limited collector interest.

ARMY: QUARTERMASTER CORPS

Each menu contained one canned meat item; one canned fruit, bread or dessert item; one B unit; an accessory packet containing four cigarettes, matches, chewing gum, toilet paper, coffee, cream, sugar, and salt; and a spoon. Each case of 12 meals contained four P-38 can openers. The inclusion of cigarettes was discontinued in 1972.

The Meal, Combat, Individual is the ration most collectors seek. Though commonly referred to as a C ration, these rations, in fact, were the replacements for the WWII-era Ration, Combat, Individual—the true C Ration. Twelve different menu selections were offered. The Meal, Combat, Individual, was designed for issue either in individual units as a meal or in multiples of three as a complete ration.

131

Rations were packed 12 to a case. The early cases, like this one, packed the meals in two layers, while later cases were only a single layer. The value listed here is for only the empty two-part container. **$25-45**

In addition to the 12-menu selection, there are further variations in the rations due to the different suppliers used through the years. .... **$15-25 each**

ARMY: QUARTERMASTER CORPS

For many collectors of Vietnam gear, the critical component of the Meal, Combat, Individual is the accessory pack. Prior to 1972, the packs were like the one shown here, and included cigarettes .. $15-20.

After cigarettes were no longer included in the accessory pack, the packaging naturally changed....... $5-10

Each accessory pack included a small bundle of toilet tissue. $1

Numerous brands of cigarettes were packaged in the rations through the years, all of which tend to be valued equally. $10-15

A small packet of coffee was found in each accessory pack. During the course of the war, various styles of packaging were used. $1

Also included in the rations were matches. $1-2

Small packages of chewing gum were enclosed in the accessory packs. Like the cigarettes, various brands of gum were used through the years. $1

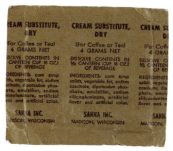

Not packed in the accessory pack, but packed inside each meal, was this plastic spoon in a plastic bag. The shape of the spoon is noticeably different from those commonly available today. $2

Not surprisingly, creamer packets were also included. . .$1

Small packets of sugar were also included in each of the accessory packs. $1

Salt, also in small paper envelopes, was included in the ration accessory packs. $1

The Opener, Can, Hand, Folding, Type 1 is commonly known as the P38. The slang term is derived from the 38 punctures which the tool required to open a ration can. The folding stamped-sheet-metal device was developed by the Quartermaster Corps's Subsistence Research Laboratory during 1942. The tool is also sometimes known as a "John Wayne," because the actor is supposedly shown using one of these devices in a WWII training film. Four of these devices were packaged in each case of rations. Because their quantities were comparatively limited, and the devices were handy, soldiers often carried them on their dog tag chains.

Today, examples in their original unopened packages are much more collectible than the can opener alone.
Opener alone. $1
Opener in original packaging $5

ARMY: Quartermaster Corps

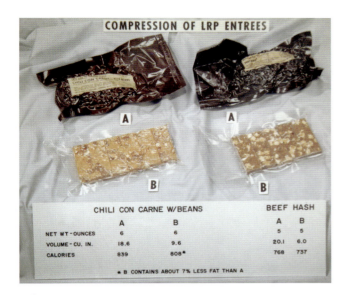

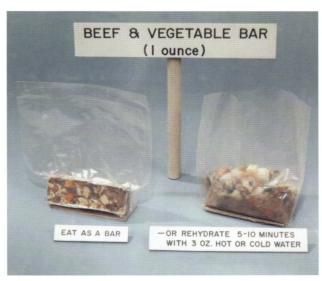

SP4 Marty, medic, 2nd Battalion, 27th Infantry, 25th Infantry Division, prepares his food. He is eating from the Food Packet, Long Range Patrol.

The Food Packet, Long Range Patrol was the result of an effort to find rations weighing less than the 2.7 pounds of the Meal, Combat, Individual. For troops operating on foot in the field for extended periods of time, the sheer weight of the canned ration was an encumbrance. Accordingly, Natick Labs (the Quartermaster Corps's research arm) developed the Food Packet, Long Range Patrol. First issued in 1964, this 11-ounce, freeze-dried ration came in eight different menus. It was intended that water be added before consumption, but it is edible without adding water. The early style, shown here, came in sophisticated packaging. The main menu item was an inner clear polyethylene bag, which also was used for reconstitution. This bag and the rest of the items were inside a dark polyethylene bag, which was inside an outer camouflage-colored polyolefin-aluminum foil-polyester bag. The eight menu selections—Beef Hash, Chili Con Carne, Spaghetti with Meat Sauce, Beef with Rice, Chicken Stew, Escalloped Potatoes with Pork, Beef Stew and Chicken and Rice—were packaged five each per case. Each menu included a plastic spoon, sugar, cream substitute, two instant-coffee packets, matches and toilet paper. **$30-50**

Very late during the Vietnam War, the Food Packet, Long Range Patrol began to be packaged in a plastic bag rather than the fabric/foil package. It is unlikely that this style of packaging made it to troops in the field prior to the United States withdrawal. Many novices confuse these with the later MRE ration.
................$10-12

These Fuel, Ration, Heating (Individual) Hexamine, replaced the WWII-style Fuel Tablets. These came in a brown/olive cardboard tube with metal end caps. $7-10

Though obsolete, the Food Packet, Survival, ST was supplied to U.S. forces during the early part of American involvement in Vietnam. It was intended for use in tropical conditions, and was intended to feed one man for three days or three men for one day. The flat rectangular can, with can opener taped to the bottom, contained starch jelly bars, chewing gum, instant coffee, instant tea, sugar and survival instructions. It was truly an emergency ration.
..................$30-40

This style of Fuel Tablet, Ration Heating was developed during WWII. It came packaged in a small re-sealable tin can. Limited numbers of these saw use in Vietnam.
..........................$3-7

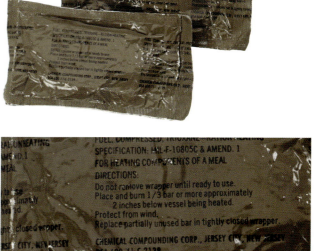

Packaged in boxes of three, these foil packets each contain a Fuel, Compressed, Trioxane bar. This easily lit and slow, evenly burning bar was intended for heating rations. Notice, like most gear, that the contract number includes a date. The values below assume three sealed packets in Vietnam-dated packaging.......................$3-5

ARMY: Quartermaster Corps

Issued one per vehicle or squad, the lightweight and portable M1950 Field Stove gave soldiers in the field a means to prepare hot food. The stove was particularly popular with vehicle crews, who had a constant source of fuel for the stove (it burned MOGAS). The two-piece aluminum carrying case doubled as pots. This stove was similar to the WWII-era Field Stove. The bottom of the carrying case is typically stamped with the not only the maker's name, but also the manufacturing date, aiding in selecting an authentic Vietnam-era stove
. . . .$30-60

For sanitary reasons, by 1966 disposable dinnerware had largely replaced the traditional field mess kit.

The traditional Field Mess Kit saw use in Vietnam. However, the lack of sufficient quantities of clean, hot water for cleaning in the field raised concerns of food-borne illness, and by 1966 most field units were using disposable dinnerware. The mess kit was made of stainless steel, and in 1965 the army abandoned the cast-aluminum knife handle in favor of a less expensive stamped one-piece mess knife. $10-25

ARMY: QUARTERMASTER CORPS

CHEST, OUTFIT, OFFICER'S MESS, M-1937
STOCK NO. 63-C-553
1952
MILLER MANUFACTURING CO.
GLEN COVE, N.Y.

When eating together, officers in the field did not use a Field Mess Kit. Rather they used the Chest, Outfit, Officer's Mess, — essentially an eight-officer Mess Set in box. Included was a teapot, coffee pot, two serving bowls, salt and pepper shakers, and eight of each of the following items: teaspoon, fork, knife, spoon, plate, bowl, cup.
. . . . $150-250

ARMY

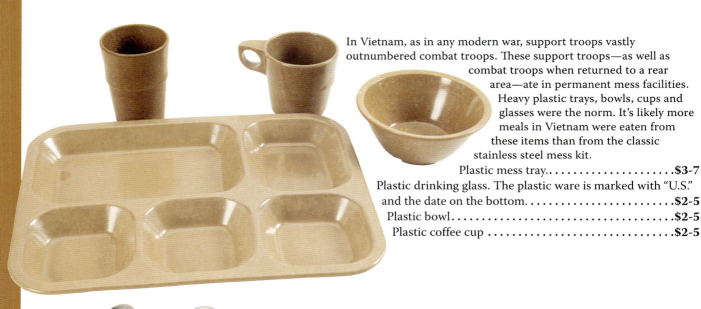

In Vietnam, as in any modern war, support troops vastly outnumbered combat troops. These support troops—as well as combat troops when returned to a rear area—ate in permanent mess facilities. Heavy plastic trays, bowls, cups and glasses were the norm. It's likely more meals in Vietnam were eaten from these items than from the classic stainless steel mess kit.

Plastic mess tray............................$3-7
Plastic drinking glass. The plastic ware is marked with "U.S." and the date on the bottom.........................$2-5
Plastic bowl....................................$2-5
Plastic coffee cup $2-5

Fork, with Medical Corps Caduceus $3-7
Knife, with Medical Corps Caduceus $3-7
Spoon, with Medical Corps Caduceus $3-7

Mermite cans were used to provide troops hot (or cold) mess-hall-prepared foods in the field. The containers were also commonly "liberated" by vehicle crews for use as coolers. Here, members of Company A, 2nd Battalion, 502nd Infantry, 101st Airborne mess from mermite cans for a hot meal in September 1967.

ARMY: QUARTERMASTER CORPS

The ubiquitous Food Container, Insulated, or as it is more popularly known, the mermite can, combined with helicopter or truck transport, allowed troops operating in the field to eat hot meals prepared at base-camp mess halls.

The mermite can is made of an inner aluminum shell, surrounded by an outer shell. The space between these two shells is filled during the manufacturing process with formed-in-place foam having a density of 1.8 pounds per cubic foot. This makes for a container that will maintain the temperature of the foods placed inside for a minimum of three hours.

The can was supplied with three removable interior containers, each with a fitted lid sealed with a rubber gasket. Each interior container had a bail to aid in its removal.

Before the unit is used to transport hot foods, the inserts are removed, and two quarts of boiling water poured inside the mermite can. Then the inserts are replaced and the cover latched. After 30 minutes, the inserts are again removed, and the hot water poured out. Hot foods are placed in the inserts, their lids installed and the inserts placed back in the can. The latches are secured diagonally on the mermite can.

If the can is to be used to transport cold foods, much the same procedure is used. The can is filled with ice, or two quarts of ice water. Obviously, both cold and hot foods cannot be placed in a single mermite can at the same time.

Over the years these containers were made by a variety of firms for both U.S. and allied forces. They are also dated on both the external container and on the inner lids. To be correct, all four dates should match. The rubber gasket around the lid is often missing. The values below assume the gasket is present.................................. **$30-60**

Signal Corps

Rapid communications, by wire and radio, played a huge role in Vietnam, and the Army's Signal Corps was the primary provider of this service, using a wide array of equipment: man-carried, mobile and fixed. In this May 1970 photo, SP4 Stephen Savasky mans an assortment of equipment in this Tactical Information Command Van at Plei Dejerang. National Archives photo.

The Signal Corps is the Army's communications arm. Telephone, radio and photography are all Signal Corps responsibilities. From the outset of American involvement in Vietnam, the Signal Corps played a key role, and as troop levels increased, its participation skyrocketed. The 1st Signal Brigade was activated on April 1, 1966, in the Republic of Vietnam. Its mission was one of the most complicated ever given to any signal unit in the history of warfare: to originate, install, operate, and maintain an incredibly complex com-

ARMY: SIGNAL CORPS

munication system that fused tactical and strategic communications in Southeast Asia into a single, unified command.

The creation of the brigade brought together three signal groups already in Southeast Asia along with other units into a single unified command, except those organic to field forces and divisions.

The mission in Southeast Asia meant providing communications to forces scattered over more than 60,000 square miles of torrid jungle, mountain ranges, and coastal lowland, much of which was under-populated and enemy-infested. One of the innovations that circumvented the difficult terrain and enemy situation was the introduction of an extensive, tropospheric scatter radio relay system, which provided numerous communications channels over distances of several hundred miles between sites. Other firsts included first use of satellite communications in a combat zone and first use of automatic, digital message and data switches.

At its peak, the brigade had more than 21,000 soldiers, with six signal groups, 22 signal battalions, and a large number of specialized communications agencies. This made it, at that time, the largest single brigade in the U.S. Army.

The stand-down of 1st Signal Brigade was almost as significant as its buildup. Caught by the reduction in forces that affected the United States pullout from Southeast Asia, 1st Signal Brigade reduced its strength from 21,000 in 1968 to less than 1,300 by November 1972.

1st Signal Brigade shoulder sleeve insignia: A shield 2-1/4 inches wide overall divided into three vertical stripes: orange, blue and orange. The blue center stripe is 1 inch wide and surmounted by an unsheathed sword, point to top, the hilt yellow and the blade forming a bolt of lightning all within a yellow 1/8-inch border. The insignia was approved on Oct. 5,1966. .... $3-5

556th Signal Co. patch: Based on Lang Bien Mountain (hence the "Mountain Men" patch reference) in Dalat, the company was assigned to the U.S. Army Strategic Communications Command and participated in five Vietnam campaigns before being deactivated in Vietnam on Jan. 26, 1972. .... $5-10

510th Signal Company patch: 510th Signal Company, 73rd Signal Battalion, 1st Signal Brigade............. $5-10

Warman's Vietnam War Collectibles Identification and Price Guide

362nd Signal Company patch: The 362nd was the most widely dispersed signal unit in Vietnam, and even stretched into Thailand. The 362nd Signal Company provided microwave radio and tropospheric long-line communications throughout the conflict region. $5-10

327th Signal Company breast pocket patch: The 327th Signal Company (Radio Relay) was a tropospheric radio unit. The unit arrived in Vietnam in November 1967 and remained for the duration.. .... $5-10

2nd Signal Group patch: This group arrived in the Republic of Vietnam in spring 1965. Prior to the creation of the First Signal Brigade, 2nd Signal was the major signal unit in Vietnam. From 1965 until 1971, the group provided Army Area signal support for U.S. combat forces in Vietnam, participated in 14 campaigns, and was twice awarded the Meritorious Unit Commendation. On Oct. 23, 1971, the 2nd Signal Group was deactivated at Fort Lewis, Wash. $5-10

AN/PRC-6 HANDY TALKIE

Work on this venerable radio began in 1945. The miniature, low-power radio provided a means of communication among infantry platoons and between these infantry units and close-support armored forces. In the jungle, range of the PRC-6 was about 300 yards, stretching to one mile in rolling terrain. No special training was required for operation of this unit.

The heart of the Radio Set AN/PRC-6 is the Radio Receiver-Transmitter RT-196/PRC-6. The FM unit operated 47 mc to 55.4 mc band. As built, the unit was powered a BA-270/U battery, which is now hard to find. The battery, connected by a single plug, provided four voltages: +1.5v, -4.5v, +45v and +90v. An optional H-33C/PT handset could be used with the PRC-6. The receiver and transmitter used 13 tubes, and a full set of spares was carried with it..............$20-40

ARMY: SIGNAL CORPS

AN/PRC-10 RADIO

Introduced in March 1951, the AN/PRC-10, or "Prick 10," was the standard U.S. portable two-way radio when the United States entered Vietnam. The 16-tube radio operated on the 38.0 to 54.9 megacycle FM band, the superheterodyne FM and transmitter sharing a magnesium case and a common antenna.

When used in backpack format, the radio was powered by a BA-279/U battery attached to the case by two spring clamps. The radio could also be mounted in a vehicle, in which case it was powered by a AM-598/U Amplifier Power Supply.

Two antennas could be used with the AN/PRC-10: the seven-section, 10-foot long AT-271/PRC antenna or the three-foot long AT-272/PRC antenna. The short antenna was preferred in Vietnam, which made the radioman a less conspicuous target for snipers. With the short antenna in place, the radio had a range of 3 to 12 miles.

The operator used a H-33B/PT handset, which was connected to the radio through a cable and 10-contact plug. The radio was furnished with a special web carrying harness.

Problems inherent with portable tube-type radios caused considerable trouble in Vietnam, leading none other than General William Westmoreland to complain bitterly about the AN/PRC-10. Accordingly, the Army replaced it with transistorized radios in 1965, and the Marines followed in 1967. . . . . **$125-175**

PRC-25 RADIO

The Radio Corporation began development of this transistorized radio in the 1950s. It used a dry-cell battery considerably lighter than the PRC-10 battery, which helped reduce the PRC-25's total weight to less than 20 pounds. The battery life was typically 20 hours. The radio was classified as standard in 1961, but production of the radio was slow to begin. A few of these early radios were sent to Vietnam in 1964 for field testing by advisors. In 1965, Westmoreland, dismayed at the number of casualties attributed to poor communications, issued an "urgent battlefield requirement" for 2,000 PRC-25s. At that time, the Signal Corps had only 1,000 sets on hand, which were destined for Europe. The radios were instead shipped to Vietnam, and production of the remaining 1,000 sets was expedited. By 1967, 15,000 of these sets were being used by U.S. and Australian troops, and an additional 9,000 by Vietnamese troops.

Combat losses exhausted the entire supply of PRC-25 antennas, forcing the Army to adapt the PRC-10 antenna for use with the new radio. The radios became a prime target of the VC, who were so successful at capturing them that they were able to issue them to their own units for use in monitoring U.S. actions.

The H-138 or H-189 Handset was used with the radio, as was the ST-138 carrying harness and CW-503 accessories bag. **$150-200**

Spc 4 Harold Collins, 2nd Platoon, Company C, 25th Infantry Division carries a PRC-25 with LS-166 external loudspeaker in the Tinh Nghia Province of Vietnam. This July 1967 photo shows the amount of gear many GI's carried during the war. National Archives photo.

ARMY: SIGNAL CORPS

PRC-77 RADIO

This radio was essentially an improved PRC-25, and but for the nameplates is externally identical. Shipments of this radio to Vietnam were begun in May 1968, where it was used alongside the PRC-25.

The PRC-77 could also be installed in vehicles by using the AM-2060 Audio Amplifier/Power Supply and the AS-1729 Antenna System. This configuration is known as the VRC-64 Radio System, and it is attached to the vehicle by means of the MT-1029 Vehicle Mount.
.... $175-250

The RT-524 was found in many vehicles in Vietnam. It is shown here installed in a M151, along with a KY-8 TSEC crypto set. This photo was taken at Landing Zone Hammond in February 1967. National Archives photo.

RT-524/VRC

The RT-524 was among the most popular vehicle-mounted radios in Vietnam. Many of these radios remained in service long after the end of the war, and like the one shown here, were subsequently repainted with CARC. Collectors prefer radios still in the original semi-gloss olive drab paint. The RT-534 is also popular with ham radio operators. $250-500

ARMY: SIGNAL CORPS

AT-1082 LOOP ANTENNA WITH WHIP

The AT-1082/PRC is a small lightweight antenna housed in a cast-aluminum case. A loop antenna is mounted on top of the case and it has an expendable whip antenna within its left side. The case is shaped to be easily handheld and serves to protect the antenna assembly when it is folded down and to protect its panel controls from accidental damage by dropping. The grooved rear cover of this case allows access to the components and provides a watertight enclosure. An instruction label that contains condensed operating instructions is secured to the cover. The controls of the AT-1082/PRC include a band switch, a fine-tuning control, and an attenuation control switch.

The antenna came with a Cable Assembly, Radio Frequency CG-2840 A/U (12-Ft). This is a 12-foot cable that provided for extending the cable connection of the AT-1082/PRC to a receiving set whenever required. It was also furnished with a Cable Assembly, Radio Frequency CG-3344/PRC (5-Ft). This is a 5-foot cable including Cap, Electrical CW-922/GRC (shield cap), for the large antenna post of the associated radio receiver, attached by cord. It is used to connect AT-1082/PRC to the receiving set.

The entire outfit was housed in Bag, Cotton Duck CW-445/PRC. This bag is for carrying and storing Antenna AT-1082/PRC, a shield cap for its output connector, and the two associated cables. Moisture- and fungus-resistant cotton duck material is used for the construction of this bag.

....$20-30

AB-1135/PRC

This antenna base was intended for use with the PRC-25 and PRC-77. The AB-1135 was made of angle iron, and was driven into the ground. The AB-591 spring base and AT-271 folding antenna were then attached to the AB-1135. . . . . $10-20

TA-43/PT FIELD TELEPHONE

The TA-43/PT is a two-wire, battery-operated field telephone that was introduced in 1956. They may be used in a point-to-point wire system or in any two-wire ring-down subscriber position of a telephone communications system. The Handset H-60 contains a push-to-talk switch that connects power for talking. The TA-43/PT does not have a receptacle for use with a headset and an associated EXT-INT switch. This unit was assigned FSN 5805-503-2775. . . . . $40-60

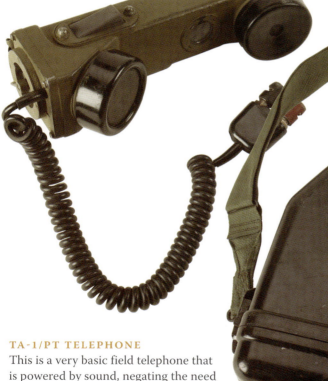

TA-1/PT TELEPHONE

This is a very basic field telephone that is powered by sound, negating the need for heavy batteries. A simple two-conductor wire is used to connect two of these phones. A miniature generator, powered by squeezing the phone, provides about 100 volts, which is used to signal the other phone to "ring," so to speak, although it is actually a buzz. A visual indicator of incoming call is also given. The phone came in a plastic carrying case. This unit was assigned FSN 5805-521-1320. . . . . $20-35

ARMY: SIGNAL CORPS

TA-312/PT FIELD TELEPHONE

More advanced than the TA-43/PT was the TA-312/PT, introduced in 1958. This battery-powered, two-wire telephone could be used in a point-to-point or subscriber telephone system. The complete TA-312/PT includes a H-60 handset with push-to-talk switch, G-42 crank generator, BZ3 clacker call signaler and canvas carrying bag with strap. An exceptionally reliable piece of equipment, this telephone was fielded by the U.S. military for 30 years. In wet conditions, the phone had a maximum effective distance of 14 miles, which increased to 22 miles in dry conditions. This unit was assigned FSN 5805-543-0012. .... $40-60

CS-34 LINESMAN POUCH WITH TOOLS

This leather pouch held a TL-29 knife and a pair of TL-13A lineman's pliers. This has been a basic issue item for Signal Corps lineman from WWII until very recently. The key here is to select items dated properly for Vietnam.. ....$50-80

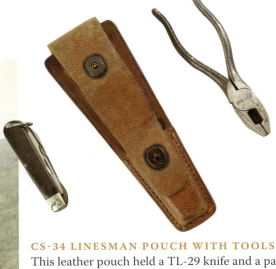

Two Signal Corps linemen of the 41st Signal Battalion, 12th Signal Group, 1st Signal Brigade gather their tools in the back of a V17A/MTQ maintenance truck. Spec 4 Harold Martin is about to put on his leather lineman's belt in this October 1969 photo.

LINEMAN'S TOOLS
The telephone lineman's tool set came in a canvas duck bag and included a pair of pole climbers, hammer, lineman's pliers and an assortment of specialized wrenches. **$75-125**

TL-29 ELECTRICIAN'S KNIFE
This knife was standard issue for many Signal Corps troops. The pocketknife had two blades—a cutting blade and a locking screwdriver/stripper blade. During Vietnam, and since, these knives were produced by Camillus, and had black plastic grips, brass bolsters and a lanyard ring. **$25-35**

BELT
The heavy leather lineman's belt was used to secure the technician to a pole while performing line work. The belts are dated on a brass button. **$25-50**

REEL UNIT RL-39
This reeling machine came with carry handles and straps, and was designed to accept the DR-8 1/4-mile spool of WD-1/TT wire as seen in the photos. It was designed to be worn, and included a crank for rewinding. The NSN for the RL-39 is 3895-00-498-8343. ..... **$30-40**

ARMY: SIGNAL CORPS

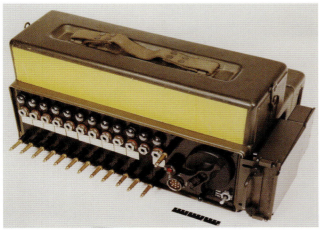

SB993/GT SWITCHBOARD
This was a lightweight portable field switchboard for emergency use in forward areas. It could handle six local battery-powered lines, and required a battery or sound-powered telephone set for the operator. The unit was assigned FSN 5805-708-2202. . . . . **$20-30**

SB-22 SWITCHBOARD
The SB-22/PT telephone switchboard was a lightweight, battery-operated field device that had 12 interconnecting voice-frequency circuits. The SB-22/PT was used to interconnect local-battery telephone circuits, remote-controlled radio circuits and voice-frequency teletypewriter circuits. Four BA-30 flashlight batteries provided 3 volts of direct current for its operation. The range of the SB-22/PT was 14 to 22 miles. The SB-22/PT consists of four basic parts: the operator's pack, the line and trunk pack, the accessory kits and the handset-headset. The switchboard unit weighed about 30 pounds, and was assigned FSN 5805-257-3602. . . . . **$150-200**

SB-3082 SWITCHBOARD
The SB-3082(V)1/GT is a 50-termination telephone switchboard designed to be mounted in a 1/4-ton truck or in a shelter. The switchboard has no cords, and connections are made by pushbutton switches. The operator can connect any two terminations, can perform preemption of any termination in use, and can establish a conference for up to six subscribers. The switchboard includes a battery charger to keep the two 12-volt emergency batteries charged. The NSN of this switchboard is 5805-00-235-5035. . . **$300-500**

Transportation Corps

The Transportation Corps controlled the bulk of wheeled vehicles used in Vietnam; hence, for simplicity, all wheeled vehicles have been included in this chapter. Logistics in Vietnam were a huge undertaking. Near ports, the military contracted with private firms to provide logistical services, and many of those used commercial vehicles, which are not discussed in this book. However, closer to combat zones, military personnel, typically operating tactical vehicles, handled transportation needs.

Today, many of these vehicles are sought-after collector's items. However, as with many collectibles, novices often purchase a vehicle that "looks" right, only to find later that their vehicle post-dates the Vietnam War.

ARMY: Transportation Corps

> **MILITARY VEHICLES CRITERIA**
> 1. **Excellent:** Restored to maximum professional standards or a near-perfect original.
> 2. **Fine:** Well restored or a combination of superior reproduction and excellent original parts.
> 3. **Very good:** Complete and operable original, or older restoration, or very good amateur restoration with all presentable and serviceable parts inside and out.
> 4. **Good:** Functional or needs minor work to be functional. Also, a deteriorated restoration or poor amateur restoration.
> 5. **Restorable:** Needs complete restoration to body, chassis and interior. May or may not be running, but is not wrecked, weathered or stripped.
> 6. **Parts vehicle:** Deteriorated beyond the point of restoration.

M38

Even before World War II had drawn to a close, efforts were made to standardize as many components as possible in order to simplify supply problems, as well as to improve the overall quality of the vehicles.

Advancements such as 24-volt electrical systems, waterproof ignition and deepwater fording ability markedly improved the combat readiness of the vehicles.

Though work was begun in 1948, the M38 (photo on previous page) was always regarded as a stopgap vehicle. The M38 was slightly larger and heavier than its WWII MB counterpart, but resembled its ancestor and used a power plant much like that of the WWII-era "Go-Devil" engine. Still, with the increased weight of the vehicle, the flathead four cylinder was underpowered.

Weight . . . . 2,750 lbs
LxWxH . . . . 133 x 62 x 74
Top Speed . . . . 55 mph
Range . . . . 225 miles

6	5	4	3	2	1
$1,000	$3,000	$6,000	$10,000	$14,000	$18,000

M38A1

Because of the increased size and weight of the M38 compared to its predecessors, performance suffered. A more powerful engine was desired. It was found in the F-head Willys "Hurricane" engine; however, this engine was taller and required the vehicle to be redesigned. This resulted in the most profound difference between a base vehicle and its A1 successor in Army military history, the M38A1, or in Willys terms, the MD. The changes were so extensive that the new version was even given its own G-number, G-758.

Willys-Overland Motors began production of the M38A1 in 1952. Though by the peak of the Vietnam War it had largely been replaced in Army units by the M151, the Marines favored the M38A1 and continued to use it. Many scholars believe the M38A1 to be the last "real" military Jeep.

The off-road performance of the Jeep was improved with the M38A1 by installing larger 7.00-16 tires, providing greater ground clearance and an improved transmission, which allowed easier shifting under adverse conditions. The more powerful F-head engine allowed the new vehicle

Photo courtesy of Evelyn Harless.

to handle the increased payload specification, as well as keep up with the rest of the faster M-series vehicle family.

Weight . . . . 2,665 lbs
LxWxH . . . . 139 x 61 x 74
Max speed . . . . 55 mph
Range . . . . 280 miles

6	5	4	3	2	1
$1,000	$3,000	$6,000	$9,500	$13,000	$16,000

Photo by Joe Shannon.

THE M170 BATTLEFIELD AMBULANCE

A stretched version of the M38A1, the M170 was designed as a frontline ambulance, though a few were used as radio trucks or airfield taxis. In the rear of the ambulance, a litter rack was mounted in the floor; an additional litter rack hung from the top bows on the right-hand side, and a third was mounted behind the driver's seat. The passenger's seat cushion was removable and was to be stored on the windshield when using the upper right litter rack. In this manner, it provided a cushion for the patient's head. Similarly, a small cushion was attached to the rear of the driver's seat, and the passenger's seatback hinged forward. An extension attached to its back formed a protective cushion for the lower litter patient's head. The spare tire and fuel can were mounted inside the vehicle in a well to the right of the passenger's seat. A droplight on a cable reel was installed near the driver for treating patients at night.

In order to accommodate the long litters internally, the wheelbase of the M170 was 20 inches longer than that of the M38A1. The front seats of the M170 were narrower than those of a standard M38A1, providing clearance for the internally mounted spare. Production stretched from 1953 to 1963 and totaled 4,155 units.

Weight . . . . 2,963 lbs
LxWxH . . . . 155 x 60.5 x 80
Max Speed . . . . 55 mph
Range . . . . 300 miles

6	5	4	3	2	1
$1,000	$3,000	$7,000	$12,500	$16,000	$20,000

M151

For many laymen, indeed for many buffs, any 1/4-ton 4x4 vehicle is a "Jeep." But the final generation of vehicle in this weight class fielded by the U.S. military had its own name, the MUTT, which stands for Military Utility Tactical Truck. Developmental work for what would become the MUTT began in the late 1940s, even prior to the adoption of the M38. Both the M38 and M38A1 were considered interim vehicles until the improved model could be fielded. (If it is any consolation, the M35 was also considered an interim design, but it soldiers on today in its 7th decade.)

Ford Motor Co. was awarded a contract to begin development of a new light utility truck. The new design would incorporate many of the latest innovations from throughout the automotive industry, both domestically and abroad. As it had been in the late 1930s when the Bantam reconnaissance car was being developed, light weight was a prime concern. To address this issue, Ford proposed various vehicle designs and materials. Conventional body-on-chassis construction, as well as unibody construction was considered, as was aluminum body construction. Ultimately, the unibody design won favor, and it was tested in both aluminum and steel construction. During trials however, the lightweight aluminum bodies developed stress fractures, and the idea was dropped in favor of a steel unibodied vehicle. The new vehicle, designated M151, was placed into production.

Weight: . . . . 2,140 lbs
LxWxH: . . . . 132 x 62.25 x 71
Max Speed: . . . . 66 mph
Range: . . . . 300 miles

6	5	4	3	2	1
$1,000	$3,000	$6,000	$9,500	$13,000	$16,000

ARMY: TRANSPORTATION CORPS

Photo courtesy of Evelyn Harless.

M151A1

The rear suspension of the M151 sometimes buckled or collapsed, particularly when heavily loaded. This was often the case when the vehicle was burdened with mounted weapons and cargo. The redesign featured new high-strength rear suspension arms, with extra bump-stops. Willys Motors began production of the improved suspension vehicle, known as model M151A1, in December 1963. In January 1964, the name on the builder's plate of the M151A1s being produced was changed to *Kaiser-Jeep Corporation*.

In 1964, a new round of bidding resulted in Ford regaining the 1/4-ton truck contract and resuming production of the MUTT in January 1965. Ford's production of the M151A1 continued through 1969.

Weight	2,320 lbs
LxWxH	133 x 64 x 71
Max Speed	66 mph
Range	288 miles

6	5	4	3	2	1
$1,000	$3,000	$6,000	$9,500	$13,000	$16,000

U.S. Army photo.

M151A2

Very few of this final production version of the MUTT were used in Vietnam. However, despite the claims of some naysayers, photographic evidence proves a handful did make it in country. The M151A2 was created because of the nasty tendency of early MUTTs to roll over during sharp cornering. The independent suspension of the MUTT often masked the oncoming threat until it was too late for corrective action.

Realizing that increased driver training alone would not alleviate the problem, another round of suspension redesign was initiated. This time the rear suspension system was completely redesigned. Rather than the independent A-frame used on the M151 and M151A1 suspension, there was a semi-trailing arm suspension system used. This allowed maximum interchangeability of repair parts with the previous designs, as well as retaining many of the advantages of the independent suspension. The improved vehicle design was designated the M151A2.

In addition to the redesigned suspension, many other improvements – including deep-dish steering wheels, larger "composite"-type marker and tail lights, electric windshield wipers and a mechanical (as opposed to the earlier electrical) fuel pump – were introduced on the new model. The new suspension gave drivers a much better indication of body tilt when turning at excessive speed, resulting in a feel more like that of a normal passenger car.

Even though the vehicle was now much more stable, some problems continued. The increased stability allowed drivers to become overconfident. As a result, even this new "safe" version was involved in rollover accidents that were just as devastating to the occupants as those of the M151 and M151A1 models.

Even though the new suspension reduced the tendency for rollovers, the Roll Over Protection System (ROPS) was introduced in 1987. The ROPS was never intended to be used on these earlier vehicles, and with a 1987 introduction date, it was never found in Vietnam.

Production of the M151A2 began in 1969. Ford was the initial contractor, but in 1971 AM General was awarded its first MUTT contract. AM General went on to win all the remaining U.S. M151 contracts through 1985.

Weight	2,385 lbs
LxWxH	133 x 64 x 71
Max Speed	66 mph
Range	288 miles

6	5	4	3	2	1
$1,000	$3,000	$6,000	$9,500	$13,000	$16,000

Photo by John Adams-Graf.

M718 AND M718A1

These vehicles replaced the M38A1-based M170 in the role of battlefield ambulance. The M718 frontline ambulance was based on the M151A1, while the M718A1 was based on the M151A2. Unlike the M170, whose body was lengthened amidships, the M718 series had extensions attached to the rear of the body to accommodate litters.

The M718 and M718A1 could each carry three litters: one in the angular lower rack, and one in each of the upper racks. The spare tire was also relocated to permit installation of the extension. The spare gas can was carried on the ambulances in a conventional liquid container bracket-mounted to the right side cowl.

Weight . . . . 2,750 lbs
LxWxH . . . . 143 x 65.9 x 71
Max Speed . . . . 66 mph
Range . . . . 288 miles

6	5	4	3	2	1
$1,000	$4,000	$8,000	$12,000	$16,000	$19,000

ARMY: TRANSPORTATION CORPS

Photo courtesy of Evelyn Harless.

M422 MIGHTY-MITE

The M422 was designed for the U.S. Marine Corps to fill the requirement of a small, lightweight, low-profile, highly maneuverable vehicle. What the Marines got was a vehicle that did just that, and gave incredible off-road performance as well. With an aluminum body, and an aluminum air-cooled 108-cubic-inch V-4 engine, the Mighty-Mite weighed just less than one ton and had superb off-road performance.

The Mighty-Mite was developed by Mid-America Research Corp., but was perfected and produced by American Motors Corp. (AMC) from 1959-1963. This was before Jeep was part of AMC.

The four-speed transmission was combined with a two-speed transfer case to shorten the driveline. All Mighty-Mites had limited slip differentials front and rear, which together with their short turning radius and light weight gave them superb off-road performance. The limited slip differentials combined with the center of gravity of the vehicle allow it to be operated normally with either one of the rear wheels missing. For this reason, Mighty-Mites were not originally equipped with spare tires.

Weight . . . . 1,700 lbs
LxWxH . . . . 107 x 61 x 60
Max Speed . . . . 62 mph
Range . . . . 225 miles

6	5	4	3	2	1
$1,000	$2,000	$3,500	$6,000	$8,000	$10,000

Photo courtesy of Daryl Bensinger.

M422A1 MIGHTY-MITE

An improved version of the Mighty-Mite, the M422A1, was built in larger numbers (2,672) than was the initial model. The most apparent differences between the two models were the stretching of the body by 6 inches and the use of an M38A1 windshield. Viewed from the side, the additional ribs stamped into the flank of the vehicle to strengthen the lengthened area are obvious. The wheelbase of the vehicle was correspondingly lengthened, resulting in the M422A1 having a 71-inch wheelbase vs. the 65-inch wheelbase of the earlier M422. The additional length of the A1 was between the front seat and the rear wheel well. The M422A1 used the same engine and transmission as the M422.

Weight . . . . 1,780 lbs
LxWxH . . . . 113 x 61 x 60
Max Speed . . . . 62 mph
Range . . . . 225 miles

6	5	4	3	2	1
$1,000	$2,000	$3,000	$5,000	$7,000	$9,500

ARMY: TRANSPORTATION CORPS

Photo courtesy of John Adams-Graf.

M274 MULE

Widely known as the Mule, this vehicle's official name was "M274 Truck, Platform, Utility, 1/2 Ton." But its versatile abilities, yet plain appearance, certainly made its Mechanical Mule name appropriate. Four companies produced six varieties of Mule between 1956 and 1970. All M274 vehicles had four-wheel drive, and the first five varieties could be driver selected to be standard two-wheel steer or optional four-wheel steer mode. However, the top speed of the Mule was only about 15 mph. Two different versions of air-cooled engines, both rear-mounted, were used over the years to power the Mules. On the first five models, the engines were pull-started with a rope. The first two models (M274 and M274A1) used the Willys A04-53 4-cylinder engine. All subsequent models used the A042 Military Standard 2-cylinder engine, which on the final version, the M274A5, was finally equipped with an electric start. The retrofitting of A0-42 engines into earlier M274 and M274A1 vehicles created the M274A3 and the M274A4, respectively.

The Army and Marines used the Mule widely in Vietnam. It was viewed as an ideal camp utility vehicle by many outfits. The first five versions were made of magnesium, while the last type (M274A5) was made of aluminum. The M274 had twice the cargo-hauling ability of a Jeep.

Weight . . . . 900 lbs
LxWxH . . . . 119 x 49 x 49
Max Speed . . . . 15 mph
Range . . . . 100 miles

6	5	4	3	2	1
$1,000	$1,500	$2,800	$4,500	$6,000	$7,500

THE DODGE M37

With the success of the WWII military Dodges, it was only natural that the Army turn to Dodge for an updated design in the late 1940s when the M-series vehicles were in their infancy.

Incorporating the lessons learned during the war and the key M-series design elements of 24-volt sealed waterproof ignition, improved weather protection, organic deep-water fording ability and standardized ancillary equipment, the G-741-series trucks, including the M37 cargo truck, were developed. The vehicles were powered by an inline 6-cylinder gasoline engine and drove through a four-speed manual transmission and two-speed transfer case.

Production of pilot models for the new design was begun in the spring of 1950. Mass production began in January 1951 with initial series production ending in January 1955.

The G-741 tooling was placed in storage until February 1958, when it was dusted off and slightly modified to incorporate minor changes to accommodate a new style transmission and relocated spare-tire mounting. The first of these new vehicles, designated M37B1, was completed in April of 1958. Except for 1960, the demands of the military, especially as the war in Vietnam escalated, were such that M37B1s were built every year through 1968. In country, the Dodges were widely used by both the Army and Marine Corps.

Weight . . . . .5,687 lbs
LxWxH . . . . .184.75 x 73.5 x 89.75
Max Speed . . . . 55 mph
Range . . . . 215 miles

6	5	4	3	2	1
$500	$1,500	$3,000	$4,500	$7,000	$9,000

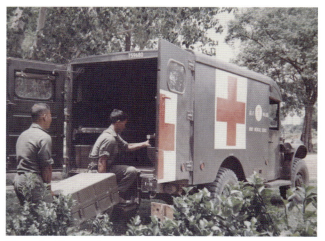

Photo by Simon Thomson.

THE DODGE M43

The M43 was the ambulance version of the M37 Dodge family. It was built on a longer 126-inch wheelbase chassis, and its suspension was designed to provide a smooth ride for its precious cargo. Both the M43 and the M43B1 came with the spare mounted adjacent to the driver's door. This spare-tire carrier was later incorporated into the B1 series of cargo trucks. No pintle hook was installed, and per Geneva Convention rules, no star or national symbol was incorporated into the vehicles' markings.

Weight 7,150
LxWxH . . . . .195.625 x 73.5 x 91.875
Max Speed . . . . 55 mph
Range . . . . 215 miles

6	5	4	3	2	1
$700	$1,700	$3,500	$5,500	$8,000	$10,000

ARMY: TRANSPORTATION CORPS

Photo by John Adams-Graf.

R-2 CRASH TRUCK

This diminutive fire truck packs a punch as big as its official title: Truck, Fire, Airplane, Forcible Entry, Type R-2. With the production total of a mere 308 units, the R-2 was never common. The bright-red color, reflective markings and unusual shape make the R-2 stand out from the ordinary military vehicle.

The R-2s were built by ACF-Brill under contract 22397 on Dodge-built, government-supplied chassis. The trucks were designed to be used in conjunction with Type 0-10 or 0-11 Foam Trucks. The Foam Trucks were to provide a path to the fuselage through the flames, and the R-2 would supply the tools and equipment to access the aircraft interior and rescue personnel. The meager 20 gallons of bromochloromethane extinguishing agent (discharged not by pumping, but with nitrogen pressurization) would hardly fight a full-fledged aircraft fire; rather, it was intended to merely get the rescuers the last few feet to the victims.

The R-2 was built on a 126-inch wheelbase Dodge M-56 chassis. The government then provided the chassis (and two batteries each) to Brill for conversion into the R-2. These conversions were completed in 1956.

At the front of the truck is the standard 7,500-pound-capacity Braden LU-4 PTO-driven winch as used on some M-37s; but in place of the standard hook, there is a grapnel. The winch was driven via a double-ended PTO on the truck transmission, the other end of which drove the 230-volt, 180-cycle, three-phase Homelite chain-driven generator mounted in the bottom of the rescue bed. This powered an electric circular saw, as well as the floodlights for rescue operations.

The glass in the cab doors is a special double-pane insulating glass, and the arms that hold the windshield open are different than those on any other M-series vehicle. The unusual sloping roof contains a Model ID-1, 11-to-20-foot A-frame extension ladder made by the Aluminum Ladder Co., accessible by opening the rear doors. Swinging the rear doors open also provides access to axes, pry bars and a variety of other forcible-entry tools stored on their interior surfaces. Also stored inside are two fire extinguishers, a Blackhawk model SB-52 porta-power, floodlight, nitrogen cylinder and the Mall circular rescue saw.

Weight . . . . 8,320 lbs.
LxWxH: . . . . 206.25 x 79 x 94.75
Max Speed: . . . . 55 mph
Range: . . . . 215 miles

6	5	4	3	2	1
$1,000	$2,000	$4,000	$8,000	$10,500	$17,500

V-41/GT SIGNAL CORPS TELEPHONE MAINTENANCE TRUCK

This truck was built on a M-56 chassis, and features a telephone maintenance and installation body specified by the Armed Services Electro Standards Agency, Ft. Monmouth, N.J. These trucks are equipped with a 7,500-pound-capacity Braden LU-4 front-mounted, PTO-driven winch. The spare tire is carried internally in the open-top bed. The bed has a low tailgate and a center aisle, with four outward opening storage compartments on either side. The vehicle also includes a ladder rack above the bed, a water cooler mounted on the driver's side, and a spotlight mounted near the driver's door to assist in night work. The Federal Stock Number for the V-41/GT is 2320-392-3703. Although the V-41/GT was listed in government manuals as early as February 1952, its specification, MIL-T-10158B, was last updated on June 30, 1957.

Weight: 7,150 lbs
LxWxH: 203.75 x 73.5 x 92.75
Max Speed: 55 mph
Range: 215 miles

6	5	4	3	2	1
$700	$1,700	$3,500	$5,500	$8,000	$10,000

ARMY: TRANSPORTATION CORPS

Photo courtesy of Crooked Creek Publishing.

THE KAISER M715

In a move opposite of the infamous 600-dollar hammer, in 1965 the military opted for a militarized civilian vehicle rather than the custom-designed and built vehicles that had been the norm since mid-WWII. Needing more trucks comparable to the M37, but hoping to save money by buying a truck that was in mass production, the M715 was born. This was an adaptation of the Kaiser-Jeep "Gladiator" pickup.

The first production contract, for 20,680 vehicles, was awarded to Kaiser in March 1966. Trucks began rolling off the assembly line in Toledo, Ohio, in January 1967. Additional contracts brought the production total to over 30,500 M715-series trucks by the time production ceased in 1969.

The Gladiator tooling was used to create the grill, fenders, hood, doors and cab of the M715 family. Changes to the sheet-metal stampings included opening up the upper part of the cab and doors to accommodate the military canvas cab top. Also, the front fenders were cut out to clear the military 9.00-16 tires. The new fold-down windshield resembled the one used on the M38A1.

The last of the M715 series to be built in Toledo were 43 prototypes ordered by the Army in December 1969. These M715s were slightly improved and intended for comparison tests against the Chevrolet XM705 1-1/4-ton truck design. Unfortunately for Kaiser-Jeep and Chevrolet, neither model was accepted.

The M715 was the first M-series tactical vehicle to use primarily civilian commercial components. The cargo bed of the M715 was unlike that of any other vehicle, military or civilian.

Although built during the Vietnam era, the M715 family of vehicles saw only limited use in country; instead, the Dodge M37 family was widely employed.

Weight . . . . 5,500 lbs
LxWxH . . . . 209.75 x 85 x 95
Max Speed . . . . 60 mph
Range . . . . 225 miles

6	5	4	3	2	1
$500	$1,500	$3,000	$5,000	$7,500	$10,000

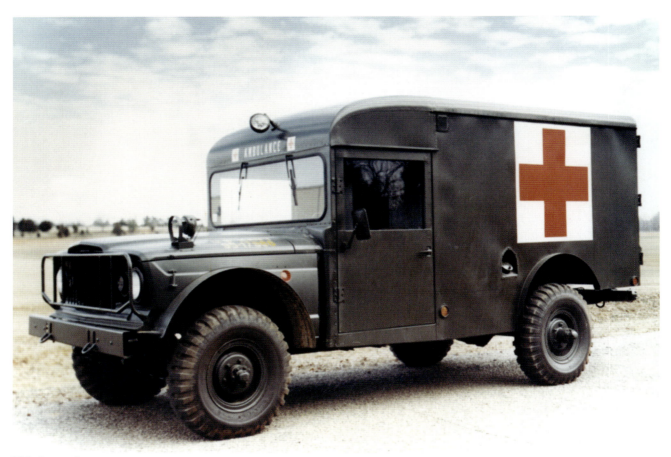

U.S. Army photo.

THE KAISER M725

This was the ambulance variant of the family. The front sheet metal resembled that of a standard M715, but on the rear was an ambulance body much like that installed on the M43 Dodge. From the firewall to the rear, everything about the M725 was different from the M715. A sliding steel door separated the driver's compartment and the rear patient compartment, which was equipped with four stretcher racks. Also provided on the ambulance body were a surgical light, air ventilators, double rear doors and a gasoline-fueled heater. The M725 was found at bases stateside, in Germany and Korea, but only a handful were used in Vietnam.

Weight	6,000 lbs
LxWxH	209.75 x 85 x 95
Max Speed	60 mph
Range	225 miles

6	5	4	3	2	1
$700	$1,700	$3,500	$5,500	$8,000	$10,000

ARMY: TRANSPORTATION CORPS

Photo courtesy of Evelyn Harless.

M726

The M726 telephone maintenance truck was built on the same chassis as the M724. On its rear was a utility box body. However, this body differed significantly from the M724, for rather than being enclosed and mounting a generator/welder, it had an open cargo area in the back with outward facing storage compartments. This bed was much lower than the M724 contact maintenance body. Some of the M726's were equipped with the 8,000-pound PTO winch and a spotlight mounted on the left corner of the cowling.

Weight . . . . .6,500 lbs
LxWxH . . . . 220.75 x 85 x 80
Max Speed . . . . .60 mph
Range . . . . 225 miles

6	5	4	3	2	1
$700	$1,700	$3,500	$5,500	$8,000	$10,000

Photo courtesy of Fred Crismon.

M35A2 CARGO TRUCK

A dual-wheeled version of the new truck was created for use primarily on roads (the single-wheel M34 being preferred for off-road operation). The dual-wheeled variant was the M35. Using dual 9.00-20 rear wheels, its bed lacked wheel wells, providing a flat floor for loading cargo, although like the M34 it was equipped with fold-down troop seats.

In the late 1950s, the military was keenly interested in developing power plants that could run on more than one type of fuel. Aware of this, Continental licensed M-A-N's "whisper engine" design, which used what Continental dubbed "the Hyper-Cycle combustion process." After extensive tests, this engine was adopted and installed in the G-742-series trucks. It was a straight-six model LDS-427-2 Multifuel engine, with 427-cubic-inch displacement. These engines are able to burn diesel, jet fuel, kerosene or gasoline, or any combination of these, without adjustment or modification. The adoption of this engine resulted in the truck being redesignated M35A1, and the slow-turning Multifuel engine required the re-gearing of the five-speed manual transmission into an overdrive configuration.

The M35A1 had a relatively short service life, being quickly replaced by the M35A2. With its improved 478-cubic-inch Multifuel engine, this would become the most common version of this family of trucks. Initially, a LD-465 naturally aspirated engine was used, but soon environmental concerns forced its replacement with the LDT-465 turbo-supercharged engine, known as the "clean burn" engine.

Most of these trucks used in Vietnam were powered by the LDS-427 or LD-465. Very few LDT-powered trucks were used in this conflict, and very few trucks with the large "NATO" lights were used in Vietnam either.

Weight 13,860
LxWxH . . . . 276 x 96 x 112
Max Speed . . . . 58 mph
Range . . . . 500 miles

6	5	4	3	2	1
$800	$2,500	$4,000	$8,000	$16,000	$20,000

ARMY: TRANSPORTATION CORPS

Photo courtesy of Fred Crismon.

M49A2C FUEL TANKER TRUCK

Fuel distribution was just as important in postwar planning as it had been during the push across Europe in WWII. Therefore, a fuel tanker was included in Reo's designs. Like the cargo trucks, various versions were built through the years. The M49, M49C, M49A1C and M49A2C each had a 1,200-gallon, fuel-tank body divided into 200-, 400-, and 600-gallon compartments. Access to each compartment was through a manhole, equipped with a manhole and filler cover assembly. Side skirts and running boards on each side of the tank body had sockets for mounting top bows and tarpaulin, with end covers to camouflage the fuel tanker as a cargo truck.

The tank body sections could be filled or emptied using the delivery pump, which was mounted in the rear compartment. The pump was driven from a power takeoff mounted on the transfer case. The delivery line gate valve assemblies and the two fuel dispensers with nozzle assemblies were provided to control the discharge of fuel. The tank body shell extended beyond the rear tank bulkhead to form a pump compartment at the rear of the body. All these trucks used a 154-inch-wheelbase chassis and were equipped with 9.00-20 dual rear tires.

While the M49 did not have provisions for towing a trailer, subsequent models did. Tanker trucks M49C, M49A1C and M49A2C were equipped with an aviation gasoline segregator kit. Tank trucks M49A1C and M49A2C were equipped with LDS-427 and LTD-465 Multifuel engines, respectively. The M49A2C did not have wheel wells formed in the bed.

Weight 14,955
LxWxH . . . . 261 x 96 x 97.5
Max Speed . . . . 58 mph
Range . . . . 500 miles

6	5	4	3	2	1
$800	$2,500	$4,000	$8,500	$18,000	$23,000

Photo courtesy of Fred Crismon.

M50A1 WATER TANKER TRUCK

Water is the most precious commodity for an army. Machines (and much more importantly, men) must have a continuous supply of fresh, clean water. Rarely are secure, safe supplies readily available. Many armies bring with them purification equipment, but even that takes time to place in operation, and distribution is yet another problem. Water tank trucks provide a means of bringing fresh water with the troops, and distributing water purified by the engineers.

The 1,000-gallon body found on the M50, M50A1and M50A2 water tankers was divided into 400- and 600-gallon compartments. Access to each compartment was through a manhole like that of the fuel tanker, but equipped with inner and outer manhole covers. Each compartment was filled through a filler cover and strainer. Delivery pump and valve controls were mounted in a rear compartment. Tank sections could be filled or emptied using the delivery pump driven by the transfer case power takeoff. Two delivery line gate valves, two water nozzles, and three discharge hoses were provided to control the discharge. An insulated heating chamber below the tank connected to the engine exhaust system by the exhaust bypass valve, and the fording valve assembly protected the tank or pipes against freezing during severe weather. Like the fuel tanker, the running board and side skirts on each side of the tank had sockets for installation of the top bows and tarpaulin with end curtains for camouflage.

Weight . . . . .14,955 lbs
LxWxH . . . . 261 x 96 x 97.5
Max Speed . . . . 58 mph
Range . . . . 500 miles

6	5	4	3	2	1
$800	$2,500	$4,000	$8,500	$18,000	$23,000

ARMY: Transportation Corps

Photo courtesy of Fred Crismon.

M109 VAN TRUCKS

The successor to the WWII-era ST-6 van-bodied truck was the M109 series. The M109, M109A1, M109A2, M109C, M109A3, M185, M185A1, M185A2 and M185A3 were all van trucks powered by the Reo OA-331 gasoline engine. The M109A2, M109A3, M185A1, M185A2 and M185A3 were equipped with the Multifuel engine. All the trucks had 12-foot van bodies mounted on subsills to raise the body and eliminate the need for wheel housings. Two side-hinged doors were mounted in the rear of the body. The right door was equipped with a latch that could be padlocked. The left door could be opened only from the inside of the body. Ladders were provided for access to the inside and roof of the van. The body had a front communication door and side windows with screens and blackout curtains. The bodies were wired for truck-supplied 24-volt DC or outside-supplied 115-volt AC power for lighting, accessories and tools. Heating and ventilating accessories were available to provide satisfactory working conditions in temperatures from 125°F to -25°F.

Various shop sets could be installed in the waterproof van body, and most were equipped with hardtop cabs. These trucks most frequently were found around semi-permanent installations.

Weight . . . . 15,291 lbs
LxWxH . . . . 263 x 96 x 130
Max Speed . . . . 58 mph
Range . . . . 350 miles

6	5	4	3	2	1
$800	$2,500	$4,000	$8,500	$18,000	$23,000

Photo courtesy of Fred Crismon.

M275 TRACTOR TRUCKS

The short wheelbase chassis of the Reo-designed G-742 series was used for some dump trucks and the M275, M275A1 and M275A2 tractor trucks. These were 142-inch-wheelbase trucks equipped with a fifth wheel assembly mounted at the rear of the chassis. Air hose and electrical cable connections for semitrailer service were stowed on the airbrake hose support that was mounted behind the cab. A deck made of nonskid plates bridged the frame between the hose support and the fifth wheel, so the operator could safely connect the inter-vehicular cables. Pioneer tools were stowed on a rack forward of the fifth wheel. Air and electrical connections were also provided on the chassis rear cross member, near the rear pintle, to permit towing of a standard trailer. The airbrake hand-control valve, used for semitrailer airbrake control, was mounted on the steering-wheel column. The M275 and M275A1 were not equipped with spare-tire assemblies or toolboxes. The tools for these trucks were stored in the cab. A gasoline engine powered the M275, the M275A1 used the LDS-427 engine, and the M275A2 used various models of the -465 Multifuel engine.

Weight . . . . 11,610 lbs
LxWxH . . . . 228 x 93 x 98
Max Speed . . . . 56 mph
Range . . . . 320 miles

6	5	4	3	2	1
$800	$2,500	$4,000	$8,500	$18,000	$23,000

ARMY: Transportation Corps

Photo courtesy of Fred Crismon.

M292A1 EXPANSIBLE VAN

These van trucks were equipped with the M4 expansible van body. The body had two rear access doors and single access doors on either side of the body. Two ladders were provided for access purposes.

The single side access doors could be used only when the van body was in the expanded position. The expansible van body was designed to expand, under tactical conditions, to about twice the volume it enclosed when in the retracted or traveling position. This was achieved by expanding side panels, actuated by expanding and retracting mechanisms, and counterbalanced hinged roof and floor sections. All facilities, including lighting, heating, air conditioning and blackout protection were available in both the expanded and retracted positions.

Four windows, equipped with brush guards, insect screens and sliding blackout panels, were located in each side panel. Two stationary windows were located in the rear doors. An opening designed to accommodate intercommunication facilities, normally covered by a removable plate, was located on the left rear panel toward the top. The telephone entrance jack and the auxiliary power cable entrance were located on the left rear panel near the bottom. The pioneer tool bracket and power cable entrance receptacle were located on the right rear panel. A bonnet, extending from the front panel of the van, housed the two heating units and the air-conditioning unit. The electrical system included a 24-volt DC circuit for vehicular light operation, and 110-volt and 208-volt circuits for auxiliary equipment operation. The high voltage was supplied by a M200 trailer-mounted generator towed by the van truck.

The M292 was powered by the gasoline engine, the M292A1 by the LDS-427 engine, and the M292A2 by the -465 Multifuel engine. All these trucks used a 190-inch-wheelbase chassis and were equipped with 9.00-20 dual rear tires. These trucks frequently housed electronic equipment, and most commonly were found in clusters of two to four around semi-permanent installations.

Weight . . . . .25,110 lbs
LxWxH . . . . 322 x 96 x 131
Max Speed . . . . 56 mph
Range . . . . 500 miles

6	5	4	3	2	1
$800	$2,500	$4,000	$8,500	$18,000	$23,000

Photo courtesy of Memphis Equipment Co.

M342A2 DUMP TRUCK

A major shortcoming of the WWII-era CCKW-based dump truck was its susceptibility to overloading due to its bed having more cargo capacity than it had the strength to support. As a result, the new generation of dump trucks, the Reo-based M47 and M59, were produced with a short wheelbase chassis, and had shorter beds to prevent this problem. In April 1953, however, Army Field Forces Board No. 2 tests reported that the M47 and M59 trucks were too small to accommodate a squad of combat engineers with full equipment, as desired. A secondary complaint was that they were too difficult to load and discharged their loads too close to the rear axle. Because it was impossible to correct these defects without a redesign, in February 1954, the Ordnance Corps began a sub-project for the development of a new dump truck with an 11-foot body, to be designated the XM342.

Unlike the M47 and M59, which had one lift cylinder each, the M342 was equipped with two hydraulic hoist cylinders. The M342 used a 154-inch-wheelbase chassis and was equipped with 9.00-20 dual tires.

Weight . . . . .15,665 lbs
LxWxH . . . . 260 x 96 x 105
Max Speed . . . . 56 mph
Range . . . . 320 miles

6	5	4	3	2	1
$800	$2,500	$4,500	$9,000	$18,000	$25,000

Photo courtesy of TacticalTruck.com.

M756A2 PIPELINE CONSTRUCTION TRUCK

The M756A2 pipeline construction featured a body and auxiliary equipment mounted on a modified M45A2, 2-1/2-ton, 6x6, Multifuel-engine-equipped vehicle chassis with dual 9.00-20 rear wheels.

The truck featured an open-top metal body with a wood-metal reinforced flat bed. The body was equipped with a winch and cab protector, rear-mounted winch, two gin poles for constructing an A-frame, two 24-volt flood lights, a tailboard roller, a custom-made toolbox, and stiff leg jacks for providing additional vehicle support. A cargo body tarpaulin with end curtains supported by top bows provided weather protection for personnel and equipment. Front and side cargo body panels, removable for side loading, supported the top bows. The side cargo racks had built-in troop seats that allowed the truck to double as a personnel carrier. The body floor was equipped with provisions for mounting two sheaves, one located at the rear and the other toward the front of the body floor slightly off-center. Gin-pole brackets were provided on each side of the body side frames for securing and carrying the gin poles that made up the A-frame assembly. Tailboard brackets were welded at each rear corner of the body side frames to accommodate the tailboard roller and allow for rear mounting and stowage of the gin poles.

A winch and cab protector was located between the cab and the pipeline construction body. The top portion of the winch and cab protector served as a platform to hold the gin poles during the raising and lowering of the A-frame. The rear winch held 300 feet of 1/2-inch cable with a maximum capacity of 20,000 pounds on the first layer of cable. The Seabees made extensive use of these trucks.

Weight: . . . . .16,960 lbs
LxWxH: . . . . 305 x 97.8 x 109.7
Max Speed: . . . . 58 mpg
Range: . . . . 500 miles

6	5	4	3	2	1
$800	$2,500	$4,500	$9,000	$18,000	$25,000

Photo courtesy of Dick Adelman.

530B PUMPER

No less than six versions of this fire truck were built on the Reo-designed chassis. The first was the class 530, which was produced in rather small numbers, and had a front-mounted pump. The 530B, shown here, was developed in the late 1950s using the M-44 single-rear-wheel chassis and a gas engine, as did the 530A. Only now the pump was amidships mounted (driven by a transfer case PTO) and the apparatus bed had compartments in which to stow the gear.

By late 1964, the 530B fire trucks were being built on a chassis with single 11.00-20 rear tires and the new Multifuel engine.

Later production trucks used the dual-rear-wheel chassis with the Multifuel engine like the one in the photo.

With helicopters becoming widely used in Vietnam, the Army needed to add aircraft crash and rescue to the firefighters' responsibilities. To aid in this, the truck was again updated, becoming the 530C. Improvements included replacing the 500-GPM Hale pump with a 750-GPM Waterous, adding a pump and roll feature, and the addition of a Feecon combination water-and-foam deck gun. Though appearing identical to the 530B, the body also changed slightly, becoming a couple inches taller.

The 530B and 530C saw extensive service in Vietnam, serving as base fire apparatus at most installations. Military fire service is a Corps of Engineers responsibility, so these trucks were crewed by and issued to engineer troops, who were then attached to other units.

Weight:. . . . . 16,960 lbs
LxWxH: . . . . 272 x 96.6 x 107.2
Max Speed: . . . . 58 mph
Range:. . . . . 500 miles

6	5	4	3	2	1
$800	$2,500	$4,500	$9,000	$18,000	$25,000

Photo courtesy of TacticalTruck.com.

M54A2 FIVE-TON CARGO TRUCK

The genesis for the postwar 5-ton 6x6 can be found in the June 1945 Cook Board Report, and was affirmed by the November 1945 Stillwell Board Report, more properly known as the War Department Equipment Board, chaired by General Joseph "Vinegar Joe" Stillwell. Both boards intended a design to have a 5-year life span, and the 1950 Army Equipment Board anticipated that the design would be replaced by cross-country carriers based on the T-51 design. Ultimately, however, various manufacturers continued production of the basic design until the 1980s, in spite of its originally planned life span.

International Harvester's design was selected for the "interim" vehicle, with one of the deciding factors being IH's engine choice: the Continental R6602. Continental Engines had previously tooled for a production of 3,000 units per month, an important consideration during the tense times of the Korean Conflict.

However, in early 1959, OTAC (Ordnance Tank Automotive Command) decided that the Mack ENDT-673 diesel engine would be tested in the M54 truck.

The ENDT-673 was basically a commercial engine of 211 gross brake horsepower at 2,100 revolutions per minute. It was a turbo-supercharged, 6-cylinder, valve-in-head, water-cooled compression-ignition (diesel) engine.

In June 1962 the new generation of trucks powered with this engine was classified Standard A as the M54A1.

The installation of the ENDT-673 was short lived, for after only a year it was decided to use Multifuel engines wherever possible in the tactical vehicle fleet. For the 5-ton, the engine chosen was the LDS-465-1A. With the Multifuel engines installed, the model suffixes changed to A2.

Weight . . . . 19,800 lbs
LxWxH. . . . . 299 x 97.8 x 117.5
Max Speed . . . . 54 mph
Range . . . . 300 miles

6	5	4	3	2	1
$1,800	$3,500	$7,500	$16,000	$22,000	$28,000

Photo courtesy of Memphis Equipment Company.

M51A2 DUMP TRUCK WITH WINCH

As was often the case in WWII, postwar-era dump trucks based on the 2-1/2-ton 6x6 chassis proved too light for many jobs. Therefore, a dump version was envisioned from the outset as part of the new 5-ton 6x6 family. This vehicle, designated the Truck, Dump, 5-ton, 6x6, was built on a 167-inch-wheelbase chassis. It was equipped with 11.00-20 tires and dual rear wheels. A 5-cubic-yard capacity dump body and twin-cylinder hoist assembly were mounted on the rear of the chassis.

Like the cargo trucks, the dumps went through a series of engine upgrades through the years, their original Continental R6602 gas engines first being replaced with Mack diesels and then later the Multifuel engine. These trucks were equipped with troop seats and bows, allowing them to double as troop transports.

Weight 22,700
LxWxH . . . . 281.5 x 97.8 x 110.5
Max Speed . . . . 54 mph
Range . . . . 477 miles

6	5	4	3	2	1
$1,800	$4,000	$8,000	$17,000	$23,000	$29,000

Photo courtesy of Joe Shannon.

M52A2 TRACTOR TRUCK

Used primarily by transportation companies and to a lesser extent by engineer and armored units, the M52-series vehicles were medium duty, off-road-capable truck tractors.

The 5-ton, 6x6, tractor truck M52 had a 167-inch wheelbase with 11.00-20 tires and dual rear wheels. A fifth-wheel assembly, approach plates and deck plate, suitable for hauling trailers, were mounted on the rear of the chassis. Tractor-to-trailer brake hoses and connections were mounted behind the cab.

Though conversion of these tractors to diesel power did not initially have the same priority as the conversion of cargo and dump trucks, eventually they were re-powered as well. The R6602 gas engine was supplanted by the Mack diesel, which in turn gave way to the LDS-465 Multifuel engine.

Weight . . . . 17 840 lbs
LxWxH . . . . 258 x 97.8 x 103.75
Max Speed . . . . 53 mph
Range . . . . 477 miles

6	5	4	3	2	1
$1,800	$4,000	$8,000	$17,000	$23,000	$29,000

ARMY: TRANSPORTATION CORPS

M328 BRIDGE TRUCK

Rivers present natural defensive lines and formidable obstacles to advancing armies. Consequently, considerable effort has been placed into the development of portable bridging equipment. One such piece of equipment is the 5-ton, 6x6, M328 bridge truck. With its 215-inch wheelbase, 14.00-20 tires, and dual rear wheels, this is one of the largest members of the 5-ton 6x6 family. Incidentally, it was also one of the last gasoline-powered vehicles used by the U.S. Army.

It was equipped with a stake body especially designed to carry bridge-building materials and equipment such as the M4T6 float bridge or class-60 bridge sections. The truck stake racks could be removed if needed to transport extra-wide loads.

The bed of the M328 bridge transporting truck was 20 feet long and 7 feet wide. A roller built into the rear edge of the bed was used to ease loading and unloading of bridging equipment. Two hand-operated winches on the left underside of the body and two identical winches under the rear of the body were used to secure loads to the truck. The beds for these trucks were built by Hobbs, Perfection, Metro Engineering and Gresham.

Weight . . . . 28,880 lbs
LxWxH . . . . 373 x 114 x 113
Max Speed . . . . 52.6 mph

6	5	4	3	2	1
$800	$1,800	$4,000	$8,000	$17,000	$23,000

U.S. Army photo.

M123A1C TRUCK TRACTOR

Until recently, tanks have been relatively slow moving. The also have been, and still are, expensive to operate, both in terms of fuel and maintenance. Every hour driven requires multiple hours of service. For these reasons, strategists prefer to haul the tanks as near as possible to the action. To this end, and to transport disabled vehicles, some of the Army's largest vehicles have been built.

Designed and originally produced by Mack, the M123 was initially powered by a throaty Le Roi V-8 gasoline engine. Production of the M123 10-ton tractor began in 1955. The tractors had either single or dual rear 45,000-pound-capacity winches, and either low- or high-mounted fifth wheels. Mack had built a total of 392 gas-powered trucks when production stopped in 1957.

In June 1965, Consolidated Diesel Electric Co. was awarded a contract for the first of what would be almost 3,000 diesel-powered versions of this truck. Known as the M123A1C, the truck used the same Mack axles and combination transmission and transfer case, but the engine now was the V8-300 Cummins. In June 1968, Mack re-entered the picture, receiving a contract to build 420 M123A1C trucks. At the same time, it was also awarded a contract to remanufacture 210 of the gas-engine-driven trucks into diesel-powered vehicles.

The fifth wheels on these trucks accept 3.5-inch kingpins, and thus will not couple to normal semi-trailers. The trucks are so large that in many jurisdictions special permits are needed for operation on public roads.

Weight . . . . 29,100 lbs
LxWxH . . . . 280 x 114 x 108
Max Speed . . . . 45 mph
Range . . . . 350 miles

6	5	4	3	2	1
$2,500	$6,200	$9,000	$22,000	$31,500	$40,000

Photo courtesy of Jeff Rowsam.

GOER

The desire to move large volumes of cargo over terrain generally considered impassable led to this unorthodox truck design. In 1956, the United States Armor Board began considering large-wheeled earthmovers as a basis for a possible new series of trucks.

Caterpillar was awarded a $5 million contract in 1960 to design, develop and build eight 8-ton cargo trucks. These test vehicles were delivered in 1961 and 1962. In June 1962, two 10-ton wreckers and two 2,500-gallon tankers were added to the contract as well.

In May 1963, a contract for 23 service-test vehicles was awarded to Caterpillar. Sent to Germany in 1964 for extensive troop trials, then stored until 1966, they were ultimately sent to Pleiku, Vietnam, to support the 4th Infantry Division. Once in Vietnam, the GOER quickly proved its merit, being highly reliable and operating where no other vehicle could go.

Based on the positive reports from Southeast Asia, Caterpillar Tractor Co. was awarded a production contract in May 1971. This contract was for the purchase of 812 M520 cargo vehicles, 117 M553 wreckers and 371 M559 tankers. Production began immediately, with final deliveries being made in June 1976.

The GOER consisted of a front and a rear section connected by an articulated joint that permitted lateral oscillation up to 20 degrees and a steering angle up to 60 degrees.

The forward section held the cab, with seats for the driver on the left and the vehicle commander to his right, and the engine behind the crew area. Power from the engine drove the vehicle via the six-speed transmission. The front-wheel drive was full time, and the rear wheels were automatically driven in first and second gears but were automatically disconnected as the transmission shifted from second to third gear.

The cargo bed had side and rear doors to allow rapid discharge of cargo. The doors had watertight seals to preserve the GOER's swimming ability. The large cargo area could hold a CONEX container and two pallets.

Amazingly, these huge vehicles were fully amphibious. Water propulsion was via their wheels.

Weight: . . . . 25,430 lbs
LxWxH: . . . . 380 x 108 x 133.5
Max Speed: . . . . 30 mph
Range: . . . . 300 miles

6	5	4	3	2	1
$5,000	$12,000	$15,000	$20,000	$25,000	$35,000

ARMY: Transportation Corps

U.S. Army photo.

LARC-V

The World War II-era DUKW was very successful at moving cargo from supply ships to points inland without port facilities, but the Army wanted something with greater capacity. The LARC filled this role. The "Lighter Amphibious Resupply Cargo" was far larger than the DUKW. Two different firms, Consolidated Diesel Electric and LeTourneau-Westinghouse, built slightly different versions of the LARC-V.

The engine was located at the rear of the hull and drove the vehicle through an automatic transmission. The entire body and hull were made of aluminum and looked more like a wheeled barge than a floating truck. The cargo area was the large flat space on the center deck, and side curtains were installed to protect cargo from rough surf.

The upper front of the vehicle held a crew cab that could be enclosed with either a hard or soft top. The truck's hydraulic power steering was controlled from the center of the cab. The engine was mounted in the rear of the vehicle, with the bell housing toward the front of the vehicle. A single-speed transmission was connected to the two-speed transfer case, which drove the four wheels using right-angle drives and planetary hubs. The vehicle was quite complex and required extensive training to operate properly.

The LARC-V was powered by a V8-300 Cummins diesel engine similar to the engine in the M123A1C tractor. The vehicles had a rated load capacity of 5 tons.

Weight . . . . 19,000 lbs
LxWxH . . . . 420 x 120 x 122
Max Speed on land . . . . 30 mph
Max Speed on water . . . . 9.5 mph
Range . . . . 250 miles

6	5	4	3	2	1
$8,000	$16,000	$18,000	$25,000	$32,000	$45,000

V-100 / M706 COMMANDO

Photos of the Cadillac Gage V-100 most often show the vehicle on convoy escort duty in Vietnam. However, a more common, albeit less glamorous, role was that of base security vehicle.

First tested in June 1962, the Cadillac Gage V-100 used many components "borrowed" from other military vehicles. The Chrysler 361 V-8 that powered it was also used in the M113. The axles beneath this armored 4x4 were similar to the axles used on M35 cargo trucks, with the addition of locking differentials.

The 14.00-20 tires, however, were of a special type, with special tread and of a run-flat design. "Commando" was even molded into the sidewalls of the tires. A 10,000-pound-capacity hydraulically operated winch was mounted internally at the front of the vehicle. The fenders on the pilot models were cut out in an angular manner, whereas later vehicles had rounded fenders. There was no provision for deepwater fording because the vehicles were completely amphibious without preparation.

The turret mounted various combinations of machine guns, such as a pair of .30-caliber guns, or one .30- and one .50-caliber, or 7.62mm machine guns instead of the .30s.

Known to the Air Force as the V-100, but standardized by the Army as the M706, the production vehicles differed in detail from the XM706. One vision block and firing port on each side were deleted, and the roof hatches for the driver were raised slightly above the surface of the hull.

Weight: . . . . .13,300 lbs
LxWxH: . . . . 224 x 89 x 96
Max Speed: . . . . 80 mph
Range: . . . . 400 miles

6	5	4	3	2	1
$7,000	$20,000	$30,000	$45,000	$55,000	$65,000

ARMY: Transportation Corps

XM706E2 COMMANDO

The XM706E2, which was popular with the Air Force, is essentially a M706 with an armored box in place of the turret, much like the relationship between the earlier M8 and M20 armored cars.

Procurement of the Commando series of vehicles began in 1964, with many of them destined for Vietnam. The first units produced retained the angular fender cutouts of the prototypes, but soon gave way to the rounded fender cutouts. Once in country, these vehicles saw extensive use by security personnel, both around camp and as convoy escorts.

Weight	13,300 lbs
LxWxH	224 x 89 x 96
Max Speed	80 mph
Range	400 miles

6	5	4	3	2	1
$7,000	$20,000	$30,000	$45,000	$55,000	$65,000

Army Publications

The Department of Defense made available literally thousands of different types of publications to U.S. Army personnel in Vietnam. These ranged from technical operation manuals to periodicals that contained both news and entertainment. Some, like the technical manuals, were intended to be permanent records and kept with the equipment, while others, just like today's newspapers, were intended to be disposable.

Today, many of the technical manuals (TM), which dealt with equipment, and field manuals (FM), which deal more with operational and strategic techniques, are sought by collectors. For example, a collector owning the Field Stove might be interested in the operator's manual for the stove, but also the messing procedures to feed troops.

Newspapers and magazine published for distribution to troops in Vietnam provide the collector with a link to the lives of soldiers in the war zone. In contrast to the manuals mentioned above, these publications were intended to be disposable. So, even though most of these publications were produced in large numbers, many of them are hard to find today.

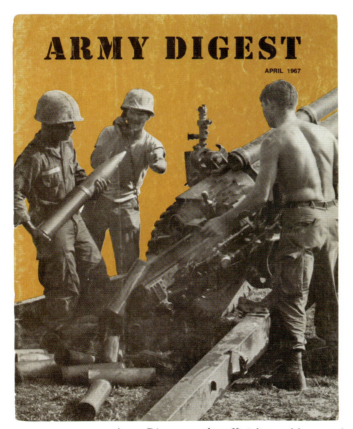
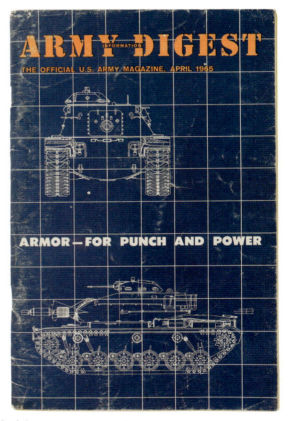

Army Digest was the official monthly periodical of the Army. In June of 1971 the name of the magazine was changed to *Soldiers*. The magazine typically contained six to eight articles about U.S. troops and equipment, oftentimes in Vietnam. Of particular interest to most GIs serving in the field was the inside rear cover, which was a full-page photo of an attractive young lady. $3-8

ARMY: PUBLICATIONS

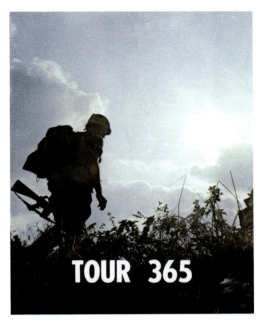

Tour 365 was an authorized publication of the U.S. Army, Vietnam. It was published under the supervision of the Information Officer, USARV, semi-annually for distribution to soldiers returning to the United States upon completion of their tour. Many soldiers discarded these immediately upon receipt. Several different editions exist, and this is the Winter 1968 edition. $25-35

A new edition of *Tour 365* was published in the summer of 1970. Probably because of the large numbers of troops leaving Vietnam at this time, this edition seems to be the one that turns up most often. $15-25

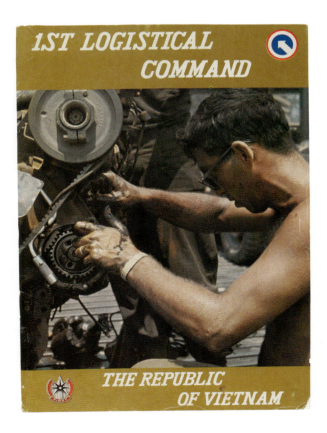

This 1st Logistical Command, Republic of Vietnam publication was a soldier's souvenir piece produced as a single issue in magazine format in 1968. It was 45 pages and printed on heavy stock, with extensive use of color and B&W photos, illustrations and soldier art. The magazine was produced as an authorized publication through the information office of the 1st Logistical Command.

The units that make up the "1st Log" were the U.S. Army troops that provided the "bullets, beans and boots" to the troops throughout Viet Nam. The magazine highlights the day-to-day operations of the various units in country at the time. Operation of port facilities, ammunition resupply, equipment maintenance, fuel and oil delivery are illustrated. Produced in a relatively small quantity, the few copies issued in country that were carried or sent home in good condition are now collectible. $40-60

Uptight US Army in Vietnam was published quarterly from 1968 through 1971 for servicemen In Vietnam. . . . **$25-35**

Hi-Lite was a magazine briefly published by the U.S. Army Support Command, Saigon. Today issues are difficult to locate. **$40-50**

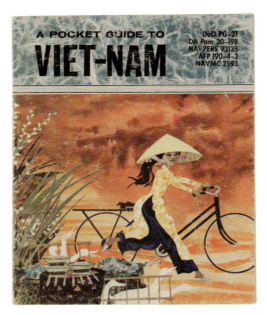

The *Pocket Guide to Vietnam* was first published in 1962. The 131-page book gave troops deploying to Vietnam an overview of the Vietnamese people, their culture and history, and their language. It was designated Department of Defense publication PG-21, and measured about 5-3/8 by 4-3/8 inches. **$25-30**

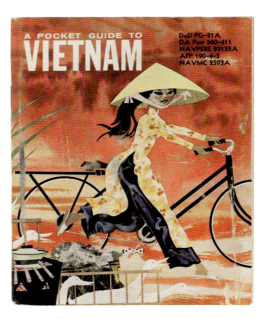

In 1966, the *Pocket Guide to Vietnam* was revised. The new edition was designated PG-21A and can be readily distinguished by the change in cover art, which now lacked the aqua band at the top. Internally, much of the material dealing with the Vietnamese culture was eliminated, making this volume only 94 pages. **$25-30**

ARMY: PUBLICATIONS

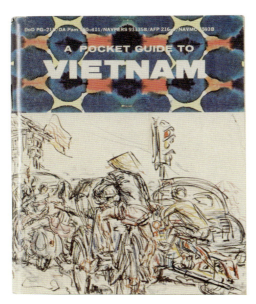

In 1970 the *Pocket Guide to Vietnam* was again revised, and was now identified as PG-21B. The cover art was completely different from that of previous editions, and the book contained a smaller translation guide. **$25-30**

The 8 Week Challenge – Your New World was the title of this small booklet that recruits were given during basic training............................... **$8-10**

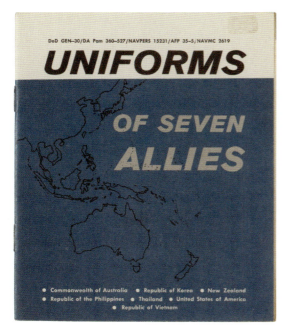

Uniforms of Seven Allies was the title of this 1967 booklet designed to acquaint American military personnel with their allies in Vietnam. It shows the uniforms, titles and insignia of rank for the armed forces of the Republic of Vietnam, Australia, New Zealand, Republic of Korea, Republic of the Philippines and Thailand. It was assigned these various publication numbers: DoD GEN-30/DA Pam 360-527/NAVPERS 15231/AFP 35-5/NAVMC 2619. .**$3-7**

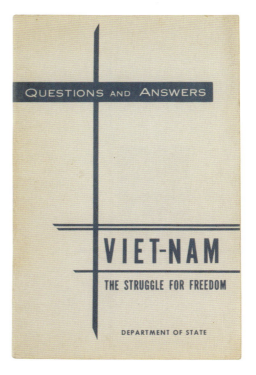

State Department Publication No. 7724 was initially published in 1964. It was not really an Army publication and provided an overview of why the United States was involved in Vietnam, and the role of our forces at that time (advisory). Later the booklet was republished by the Department of Defense as DoD GEN-8. The DoD version has a different cover........................ **$20-30**

Chien Cu: War Material Used by the Viet Cong in South Vietnam or Presumably Available to North Vietnam. This publication illustrated and described NVA and Viet Cong weapons and equipment. The text is in both English and Vietnamese. $30-50

Chien Cu (II): War Material Used by Viet Cong in South Vietnam. This publication illustrated and described NVA and Viet Cong weapons and equipment. The text is in both English and Vietnamese. $30-50

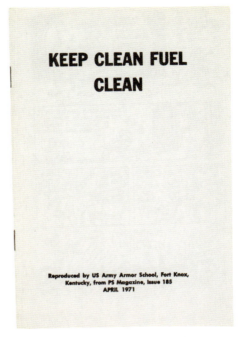

Keep Clean Fuel Clean April 1971. Clean fuel was critical for tactical operations as well as motor transport. Maintaining clean fuel under the conditions found in Vietnam could be difficult, and this pamphlet raised awareness of this issue as well as tips on effective procedures. $5-10

This pamphlet, titled *Heavy Hints for Light Packs*, came packaged inside each new M1961 field pack until 1966. The pamphlet described how to use the M1956 load-carrying equipment. $10-14

Graphic Training Aid 3-4-7 ABC-M17 and M17A1 CB Field Protective Mask Care July 1972. This was a simple and basic guide to the use of the gas mask. $8-10

Be Your Own Inspector – 5-ton trucks. The driver is the first line of maintenance on his vehicle. This booklet gave handy tips on pre- and post-mission inspections with an eye toward reducing vehicle downtime for maintenance. $10-20

ARMY: Publications

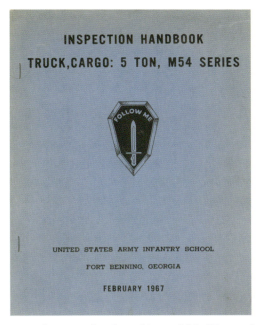

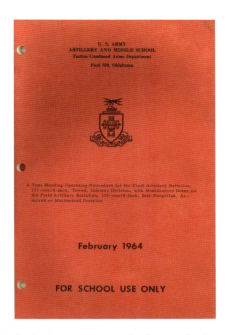

Five-ton trucks were also the subject of this 27-page book published in February 1967 by the infantry school at Ft. Benning, Ga. This photo-illustrated book covered basic operation and maintenance methods. $5-10

Each unit deploying to Vietnam had a standard operating procedure. This was derived from army regulations, field manuals and technical manuals, as well as local commands. Published editions provide a unique insight into the why and how of unit operations. $5-15

PS Magazine began in June 1951. At that time the publication resembled a newspaper, and was published sporadically. From the outset, the publication had a colorful cartoon format and featured the gruff Sgt. Halfmast and the curvaceous Connie Rod. Soon the format settled into the familiar booklet seen here, and was published monthly. Early editions are hard to find, particularly the newspaper-style one. Most of the Vietnam-era issues are reasonably obtainable. $1-4

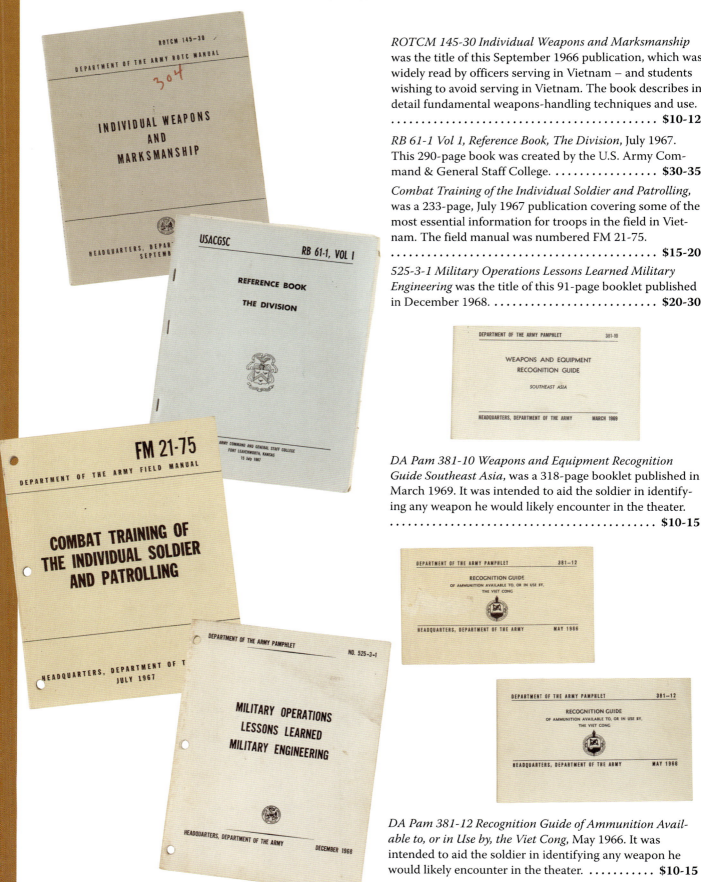

ROTCM 145-30 Individual Weapons and Marksmanship was the title of this September 1966 publication, which was widely read by officers serving in Vietnam – and students wishing to avoid serving in Vietnam. The book describes in detail fundamental weapons-handling techniques and use. $10-12

RB 61-1 Vol 1, Reference Book, The Division, July 1967. This 290-page book was created by the U.S. Army Command & General Staff College. $30-35

Combat Training of the Individual Soldier and Patrolling, was a 233-page, July 1967 publication covering some of the most essential information for troops in the field in Vietnam. The field manual was numbered FM 21-75. .... $15-20

525-3-1 Military Operations Lessons Learned Military Engineering was the title of this 91-page booklet published in December 1968. .... $20-30

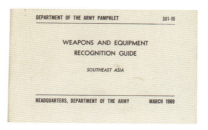

DA Pam 381-10 Weapons and Equipment Recognition Guide Southeast Asia, was a 318-page booklet published in March 1969. It was intended to aid the soldier in identifying any weapon he would likely encounter in the theater. $10-15

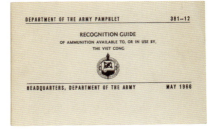

DA Pam 381-12 Recognition Guide of Ammunition Available to, or in Use by, the Viet Cong, May 1966. It was intended to aid the soldier in identifying any weapon he would likely encounter in the theater. $10-15

ARMY: PUBLICATIONS

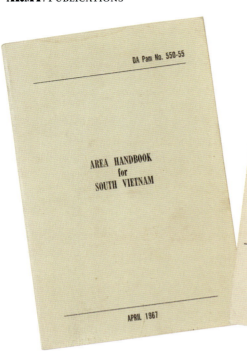
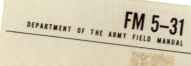

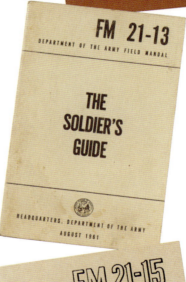

DA Pam 550-55 Area Handbook for South Vietnam, April, 1967. This is one of a series of handbooks prepared by the Foreign Area Studies of the American University. It provided a convenient compilation of basic facts concerning social, economic, political and military institutions and practices. $10-15
To instruct U.S. troops in how to improvise mines from common munitions and explosives, FM 5-31, titled *Boobytraps* was published in September 1965. . . . .$5-10
This December 1969 edition of *FM 5-34 Engineer Field Data* provides basic instruction on the movement of troops both offensively and defensively. It includes safety and survival information of various materials, including safe demolition distances. Also included are metal, wood and electrical measurements, along with mathematical equations. This was to serve as a general reference manual for all engineer units. $10-20
FM 21-13, The Soldiers Guide, describes the history of the Army, the uniform, the role of the soldier and military courtesy. It is the basic "how to be a soldier" book, and the August 1961 edition was common to many soldiers serving in Vietnam. $5-15
The name of FM 21-15, *Care and Use of Individual Clothing and Equipment*, was pretty self-explanatory. Variations of this manual have been issued since WWII, and when U.S. troops first went to Vietnam the May 1956 edition was in effect. $8-12

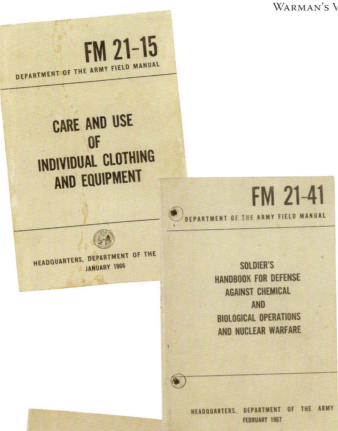

Like most army manuals, the FM 21-15 was constantly updated, and the issue commonly seen in the gear of GIs in Vietnam is this January 1965 edition. $8-12

The ability to read maps is critical to all soldiers for a variety of reasons. For this reason, *FM 21-26 Map Reading*, was published. Every soldier was expected to be familiar with the information and techniques found in this volume. $10-15

FM 21-41 Soldier's Handbook for Chemical and Biological Operations and Nuclear Warfare, February 1967. Soldiers in Vietnam, especially the famed tunnel rats, were concerned about tear gas and other irritants. Hence, many familiarized themselves with the information contained in this manual. $20-30

Officers of 2nd Battalion, 34th Armor look over a map at Fire Support Base Saint Barbara in August 1970. Training, as well as publications, built competence in map reading and a host of other tasks used by soldiers in Vietnam. National Archives photo

ARMY: Publications

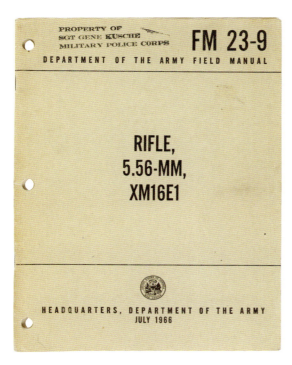

FM 23-9 was the army field manual aimed at improving marksmanship with the M16. Although this manual is still in print, for the Vietnam-gear collector, this July 1966 edition is the sought-after one.................... $20-30

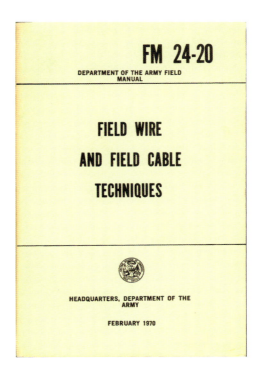

This compact 350-page manual, *FM 24-20 Field Wire and Field Cable Techniques* dated February 1970, was intended for use by Signal Corps linemen. It detailed various equipment and techniques of field-telephone installation and maintenance.................................$5-10

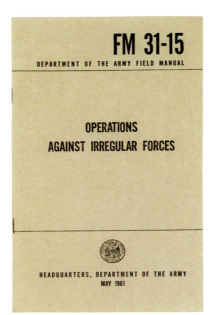

FM 31-15 Operations Against Irregular Forces was the title of this May 1961 manual intended to aid commanders and staff of combined arms in operations against organized guerrilla units and underground forces. Among other things, the manual describes the tactics and techniques used by insurgents........................... $10-20

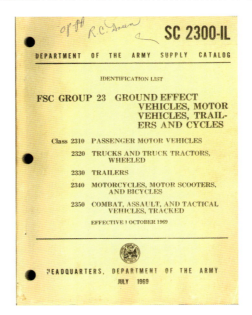

This July 1969 *Supply Catalog* lists items in Federal Supply Class 23, which covers motor vehicles and trailers. Listed are all the types of vehicles considered standard items, brief descriptions, including the Federal Stock Numbers for ordering, and a few illustrations............. $20-40

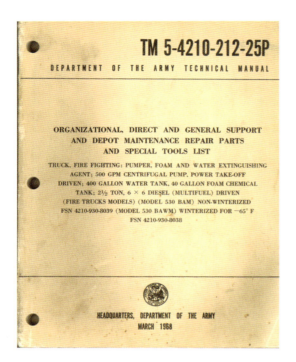

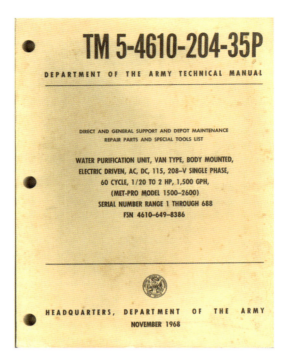

A broad range of technical manuals was produced, each with their unique publication number. Pub numbers ending in "P" were parts books, such as this TM 5-4210-212-25P, which is the parts breakdown for a fire truck on a standard military 2-1/2-ton 6x6 chassis. The "5" prefix to the TM number indicates it is Corps of Engineers equipment. $5-10

TM 9-1005-223-10 Operator's Manual for Rifle, 7.62-MM, M14, W/E; Rifle, 7.62-MM, M14A1, W/E; Bipod, Rifle, M2 (March 1972). This was the final Vietnam-era edition of the operator's manual for the M14 rifle. By this time the rifle was seeing only limited use with U.S. troops, but was widely used by allied forces.. . . . . $5-10

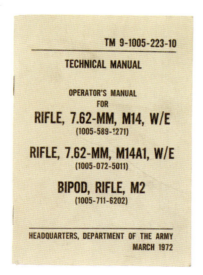

TM 9-1005-223-10 Operator's Manual for Rifle, 7.62-MM, M14, W/E; Rifle, 7.62-MM, M14A1, W/E; Bipod, Rifle, M2 (March 1972). This was the final Vietnam-era edition of the operator's manual for the M14 rifle. By this time the rifle was seeing only limited use with U.S. troops, but was widely used by allied forces.. . . . . $5-10

Operation and Preventive Maintenance M16A1 Rifle. Styled along the same lines as *PS* magazine, this 30-page training manual was done in a comic-book format and included information on stripping and cleaning the rifle, clearing a jam and other basic principles. Published in July 1969. . . . . $10-12

ARMY: Publications

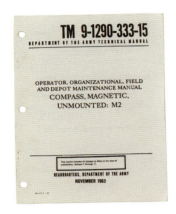

The pocket-sized *Operator's Manual for the M60 Machine Gun* had a red cover and was numbered TM9-1005-224-10. This manual was supplied with the weapon beginning in October 1970.................................$1-2

TM 9-1290-333-15 Operator's, Organizational, Direct Support, General Support and Depot Maintenance (Including Repair Parts and Special Tools List): Compass, Magnetic, Unmounted: M2, Nov. 7 1963. Along with map reading, the proper use of a compass is a critical skill for soldiers, not only for survival, but also for locating artillery fire and air support. Accordingly, the army published this detailed manual on the use and maintenance of a compass...$5-10

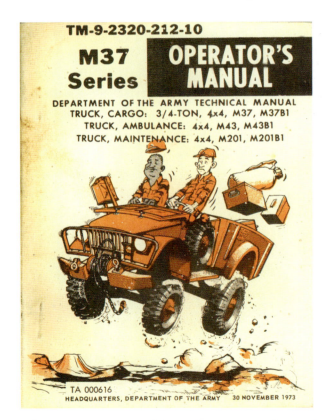

The maintenance manual for the 10-ton 6x6 tractor, used in Vietnam for tank and heavy equipment recovery and transport, was TM 9-2320-206-20............... $20-40

As the Vietnam war wound down, the army experimented with comic-book styling for technical manuals, such as this 1973 TM 9-2320-212-10 operator's manual for the M37-series trucks. Such styling had been successful with the *PS* magazine, but was not well received in the TMs, and was not widely used............................. $20-25

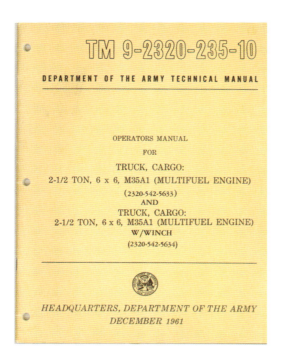

This is the December 1961 operator's manual for the M35A1 2-1/2-ton 6x6, which was in use as the earliest U.S. troops reached Vietnam; 66 pages. **$10-20**

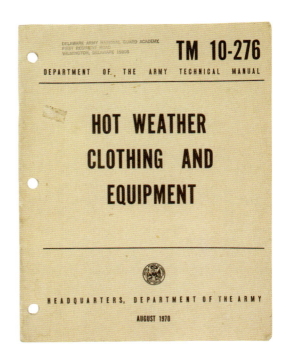

TM 10-276 Hot Weather Clothing and Equipment manual from August 1970. This manual describes each clothing item likely to have been issued to troops in Vietnam on its date of publication. Information is given on wear, use and cleaning of the item. **$5-10**

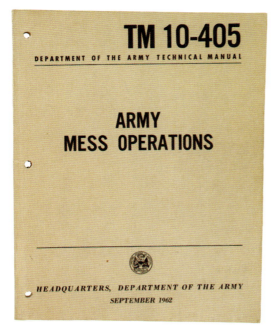

This September 1962 edition of *TM 10-405 Army Mess Operations* detailed how troops were to be fed. . . . **$10-15**

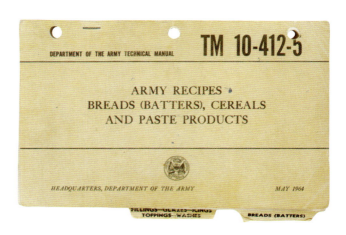

It has long been said that an army travels on its stomach, and this old adage includes the recipes contained within *TM 10-412-5 Army Recipes Breads (Batters), Cereals and Paste Products*, dated May 1964. . . . . **$20-25**

ARMY: PUBLICATIONS

TM 11-5805-201-12 Operator's and Organizational Maintenance Manual for Telephone Set, TA-312/PT and TA-312A/PT, June 1947. The TA-312 had been in service for nearly 20 years when U.S. troops began arriving in Vietnam in numbers. Each phone came with an operator's manual – which could have been published at any time during the phone's service life. $5-10

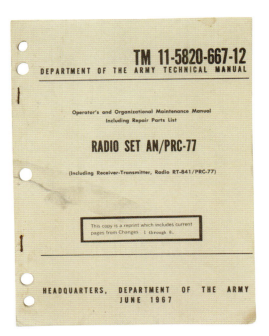

TM 11-5820-667-12 is the *Operator's and Organizational Maintenance Manual* for the familiar AN/PRC-77. Each radio was supplied with this manual, and the designated radio operator was expected to be familiar with it. $10-20

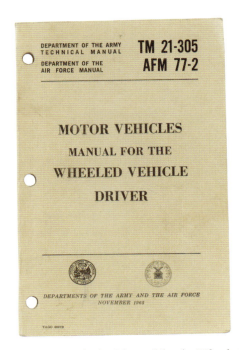

TM 21-305, Motor Vehicles Manual for the Wheeled Vehicle Driver, covered the basics of operating military wheeled vehicles. The edition widely used in Vietnam was dated November 1965. . . . . $10-15

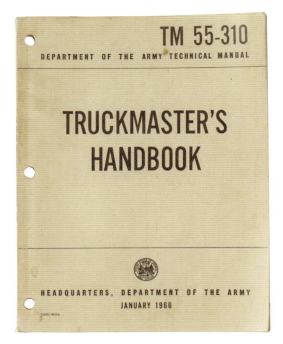

The truckmaster served as the assistant to a Transportation Company Commander. For guidance, the truckmaster turned to the 129-page *TM 55-310 Truckmaster's Handbook.* The January 1966 edition was widely used during the Vietnam War. $12-18

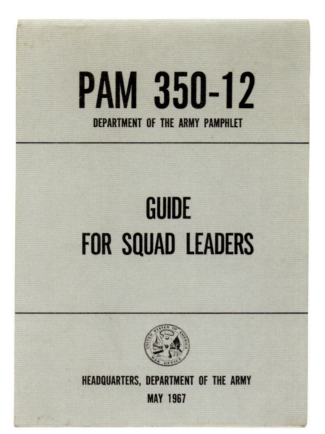

AM 350-12 Guide for Squad Leaders, May 1967. This 225-page book covers infantry procedures and leadership issues. $10-20

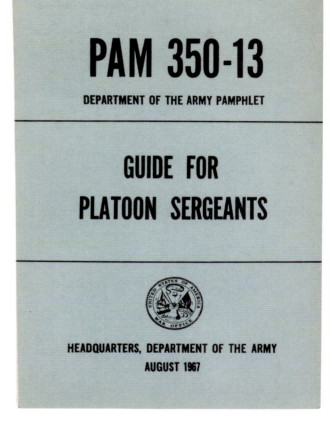

PAM 350-13 Guide for Platoon Sergeants, dated August 1967, provided new platoon leaders with insight as to what was expected of them, both from their superiors and their men. $10-20

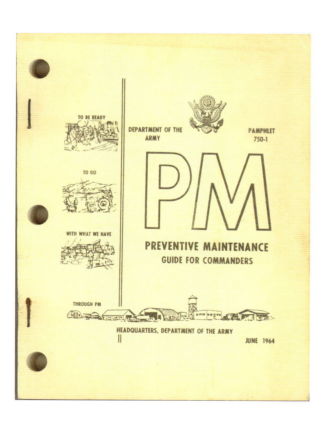

Department of the Army Pamphlet 750-1 of June 1964 was a 300-page, photo-illustrated book highlighting trouble maintenance areas on a range of equipment, from typewriters to missiles. $5-10

Insignia and Medals

Some collectors focus on patches and insignia, others entirely on medals and awards of valor. Still others view both to be only "accessories" for the uniforms they collect. Listed here are some of the most popularly examples of both insignia and medals. Because these categories of collectibles are so popular, there are many excellent books – larger than this one – that deal exclusively with each category.

Medals, awards and insignia are often reproduced. It is strongly recommended that novices considering making a significant purchase in these areas seek the advice of one or more experienced collectors, and buy only from a reputable dealer with a clearly stated guarantee and return policy. Because the trading of the Medal of Honor is illegal, it is not listed here.

VIETNAM SERVICE MEDAL
The Vietnam Service Medal was awarded to all members of the armed forces who served in Vietnam and contiguous waters and airspace between July 3, 1965, and March 28, 1973.
............................$10-15

VIETNAM CAMPAIGN MEDAL
The Vietnam Campaign Medal was awarded to any member of the U.S. or allied military forces who completed at least six months of duty in the Republic of Vietnam between March 1, 1961, and March 28, 1973. It was also awarded to any service member who, while serving outside the geographical limits of South Vietnam, provided direct combat support to the Republic of Vietnam Armed Forces for a period exceeding six months. The Vietnam Campaign Medal is considered a foreign award by the U.S. government.
.... $10-15

DISTINGUISHED SERVICE CROSS
The Distinguished Service Cross (DSC) is the second-highest military decoration of the U.S. Army. It is awarded to a person who, while serving in any capacity with the Army, distinguished himself or herself by extraordinary heroism not justifying the award of a Medal of Honor; while engaged in an action against an enemy of the United States; while engaged in military operations involving conflict with an opposing or foreign force; or while serving with friendly foreign forces engaged in an armed conflict against an opposing armed force in which the United States is not a belligerent party. The act or acts of heroism must have been so notable and have involved risk of life so extraordinary as to set the individual apart from his or her comrades. $125-175

Warman's Vietnam War Collectibles Identification and Price Guide

DISTINGUISHED SERVICE MEDAL
The Distinguished Service Medal is awarded to any person who, while serving in any capacity with the U.S. Army, has distinguished himself or herself by exceptionally meritorious service to the Government in a duty of great responsibility. The performance must be such as to merit recognition for service that is clearly exceptional. (Exceptional performance of normal duty will not alone justify an award of this decoration.) $100-150

SILVER STAR
The Silver Star is awarded to a person who, while serving in any capacity with the U.S. Army, is cited for gallantry in action against an enemy of the United States while engaged in military operations involving conflict with an opposing foreign force, or while serving with friendly foreign forces engaged in armed conflict against an opposing armed force in which the United States is not a belligerent party. The required gallantry, while of a lesser degree than that required for the Distinguished Service Cross, must nevertheless have been performed with marked distinction. $75-125

BRONZE STAR
The Bronze Star Medal is awarded to any person who, while serving in any capacity in or with the Army of the United States after Dec. 6, 1941, distinguished himself or herself by heroic or meritorious achievement or service, not involving participation in aerial flight, in connection with military operations against an armed enemy; or while engaged in military operations involving conflict with an opposing armed force in which the United States is not a belligerent party. $25-50

AIR MEDAL
The Air Medal was awarded to any person who, while serving in any capacity in or with the U.S. Army, distinguished himself or herself by meritorious achievement while participating in aerial flight. Awards may be made to recognize single acts of merit or heroism, or for meritorious service as described here. $40-75

PURPLE HEART
The Purple Heart is awarded in the name of the President of the United States to any member of an armed force or any civilian national of the United States who, while serving under competent authority in any capacity with one of the U.S. Armed Services after April 5, 1917, has been wounded or killed, or who has died or may hereafter die after being wounded in any action against an enemy of the United States $50-75

GOOD CONDUCT MEDAL
The Good Conduct Medal was awarded for exemplary behavior, efficiency and fidelity in active Federal military service. It is awarded on a selective basis to each soldier who distinguishes himself or herself from among his or her fellow soldiers by their exemplary conduct, efficiency and fidelity throughout a specified period of continuous enlisted active Federal military service, as outlined in this chapter. There is no right or entitlement to the medal until the immediate commander has approved the award and the award has been announced in permanent orders. $15-25

ARMY: INSIGNIA AND MEDALS

NATIONAL DEFENSE SERVICE MEDAL
The National Defense Service Medal was awarded for honorable active military service for any period between June 27, 1950, and July 27, 1954, or between Jan. 1, 1961, and Aug. 14, 1974. . . . .$10-15

LEGION OF MERIT
The Legion of Merit is awarded to any member of the Armed Forces of the United States or a friendly foreign nation who has distinguished himself or herself by exceptionally meritorious conduct in the performance of outstanding services and achievements. The performance must have been such as to merit recognition of key individuals for service rendered in a clearly exceptional manner. Performance of duties normal to the grade, branch, specialty, or assignment and experience of an individual is not an adequate basis for this award. $100-150

DISTINGUISHED FLYING CROSS
The Distinguished Flying Cross is awarded to any person who, while serving in any capacity with the Army of the United States, distinguished himself or herself by heroism or extraordinary achievement while participating in aerial flight. The performance of the act of heroism must be evidenced by voluntary action above and beyond the call of duty. The extraordinary achievement must have resulted in an accomplishment so exceptional and outstanding as to clearly set the individual apart from his or her comrades or from other persons in similar circumstances. Awards will be made only to recognize single acts of heroism or extraordinary achievement and will not be made in recognition of sustained operational activities against an armed enemy. $100-125

SOLDIER'S MEDAL
The Soldier's Medal was awarded to any person of the Armed Forces of the United States or of a friendly foreign nation who, while serving in any capacity with the Army of the United States, distinguished himself or herself by heroism not involving actual conflict with an enemy. The same degree of heroism is required as for the award of the Distinguished Flying Cross. The performance must have involved personal hazard or danger and the voluntary risk of life under conditions not involving conflict with an armed enemy. Awards will not be made solely on the basis of having saved a life. $50-75

ARMY COMMENDATION MEDAL
The Army Commendation Medal was awarded to any member of the Armed Forces of the United States who, while serving in any capacity with the Army after Dec. 6, 1941, distinguishes himself or herself by heroism, meritorious achievement or meritorious service. Award may be made to a member of the armed forces of a friendly foreign nation who, after June 1, 1962, distinguishes himself or herself by an act of heroism, extraordinary achievement, or meritorious service which has been of mutual benefit to a friendly nation and the United States. $10-15

JOINT SERVICES COMMENDATION MEDAL
The Joint Services Commendation Medal was awarded in the name of the Secretary of Defense to members of the armed forces who, while assigned to a joint activity after Jan. 1, 1963, distinguish themselves by outstanding achievement or meritorious service, but not to an extent that would justify award of the Defense Meritorious Service Medal. $15-20

The Armed Forces Expeditionary Medal can be earned through U.S. military operations, operations in direct support of the United Nations and U.S. operations of assistance to friendly foreign nations.

A minimum of 30 days consecutive or 60 days non-consecutive service is required for the Armed Forces Expeditionary Medal, unless the full period of an operation is less than 30 days, for which participation for the entire period is required. Personnel engaged in combat, or a duty that is equally as hazardous, qualify for award without regard for time in the area.. . . . . $5-15

Insignia

Virtually every unit in Vietnam had a distinctive insignia or patch, whether authorized or not. Some were plain and utilitarian; others were brightly colored. Shown here are but a few of the hundreds of different insignia to have been worn during the course of the war. For a comprehensive list of army units deployed to Vietnam and their histories, consult Shelby Stanton's *Vietnam Order of Battle.*

MILITARY ASSISTANCE COMMAND, VIETNAM
Military Assistance Command, Vietnam was established Feb. 8, 1962. It was reorganized on May 15, 1964, and departed Vietnam March 29, 1973. . . . . $5-10

UNITED STATES ARMY, VIETNAM
The United States Army, Vietnam was created July 20, 1965, and disbanded May 15, 1972.. . . . . $5-10

I FIELD FORCE VIETNAM
I Field Force Vietnam was created March 19, 1966, and was absorbed into the Second Regional Assistance Command on April 30, 1971. . . . $2-8

4TH INFANTRY DIVISION
The Fourth Infantry Division arrived in Vietnam Sept. 25, 1966 and departed Dec. 7, 1970. . . . . $5-10

9TH INFANTRY DIVISION
The Ninth Infantry Division arrived in Vietnam on Dec. 16, 1966, and departed Aug. 27, 1969. . . . . $6-12

25TH INFANTRY DIVISION
The 25th Infantry Division arrived in Vietnam on March 28, 1966, and departed Dec. 8, 1970. . . . . $5-10

ARMY: INSIGNIA AND MEDALS

5TH INFANTRY DIVISION
The First Brigade, 5th Infantry Division arrived in Vietnam July 25, 1968, and departed Aug. 27, 1971. .... **$2-8**

20TH ENGINEER BRIGADE
The 20th Engineer Brigade arrived in Vietnam on Aug. 3, 1967, and departed Sept. 20, 1971. .... **$5-10**

1ST AVIATION BRIGADE
The 1st Aviation Brigade was established in Vietnam on May 25, 1966, and departed Vietnam on March 28, 1973. .... **$6-12**

1ST LOGISTICAL COMMAND
The 1st Logistical Command arrived in Vietnam on March 30, 1965, and departed Dec. 7, 1970. .... **$10-15**

44TH MEDICAL BRIGADE
The 44th Medical Brigade arrived in Vietnam on April 24, 1966 and departed Dec. 14, 1970. .... **$15-20**

173RD AIRBORNE BRIGADE
The 173rd Airborne Brigade arrived in Vietnam on May 7, 1965, and departed Aug. 25, 1971. .... **$6-12**

11TH LIGHT INFANTRY BRIGADE
The 11th Light Infantry Brigade arrived in Vietnam on Dec. 19, 1967, and departed Nov. 13, 1971 .... **$10-15**

AMERICAL DIVISION (23RD INFANTRY DIVISION)
The storied Americal Division had been deactivated in 1956, but was reactivated in Vietnam by Gen. William Westmoreland on Sept. 25, 1967. The Division departed Vietnam on Nov. 29, 1971. Though assigned the number 23, the Division was known as the Americal, the name being a contraction of "American New Caledonian Division," from the South Pacific island where it was formed in 1942. .... **$6-12**

1ST CAVALRY DIVISION
The 1st Cavalry Division arrived in Vietnam on Sept. 11, 1965, and departed April 29, 1971. .... **$5-10**

1ST INFANTRY DIVISION
The !st Infantry Division arrived in Vietnam on Oct. 2, 1965, and departed April 15, 1970. . . . . **$5-10**

82ND AIRBORNE DIVISION
The 3rd Brigade of the 82nd Airborne Division arrived in Vietnam on Feb. 18, 1968, and departed Dec. 11, 1969. . . . . **$5-10**

101ST AIRBORNE DIVISION
The 101st Airborne Division arrived in Vietnam on Nov. 19, 1967, and departed March 10, 1972. . . . . . **$5-10**

U.S. ARMY ENGINEER COMMAND, VIETNAM
The U.S. Army Engineer Command, Vietnam was from Dec. 1, 1966, through March 1968 as a provisional command. From Feb. 1, 1970, through April 1972, it was non-provisional. **$10-20**

18TH ENGINEER BRIGADE
The 18th Engineer Brigade arrived in Vietnam on Sept. 20, 1965, and departed Sept. 20, 1971. . . . . **$5-10**

5TH SPECIAL FORCE GROUP
The 5th Special Force Group arrived in Vietnam on Oct. 1, 1964, and departed March 3, 1971. . . . . **$8-15**

11TH ARMORED CAVALRY REGIMENT
The 11th Armored Cavalry Regiment arrived in Vietnam on Sept. 8, 1966, and departed March 5, 1971. . . . **$5-10**

18TH MILITARY POLICE BRIGADE
The 18th Military Police Brigade arrived in Vietnam on Sept. 8, 1966, and departed March 29, 1973 . . . . **$10-15**

198TH LIGHT INFANTRY BRIGADE
The 198th Infantry Brigade (Light) arrived in Vietnam Oct. 21, 1967, and departed Nov. 13 1971. . . . . **$10-15**

199TH LIGHT INFANTRY BRIGADE
The 199th Infantry Brigade (Light) arrived in Vietnam on Dec. 10, 1966, and departed Oct. 11, 1970. . . . . **$10-15**

ARMY: PERSONAL GEAR

PERSONAL GEAR

The Army sought to provide everything that the soldier needed in the field, and in most cases frowned on GI's supplementing issue items with the own gear. Naturally, however, GI's added their own favorite items to what they carried – some of these additions being private-purchase items, others being issue items – just not issued to everyone. For the most part, the gear listed here would not be uniformly distributed among soldiers in a unit. One may have had foot powder, another may have had sunscreen, still another may have carried a private-purchase fighting knife, while others may have traded a Huey pilot for a pilot's penlight. The items in this chapter add a bit of individuality to the soldiers' equipment.

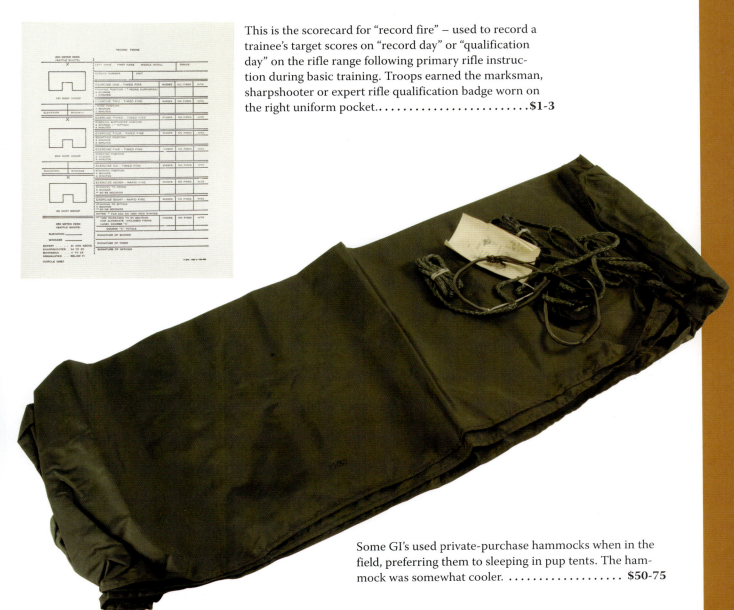

This is the scorecard for "record fire" – used to record a trainee's target scores on "record day" or "qualification day" on the rifle range following primary rifle instruction during basic training. Troops earned the marksman, sharpshooter or expert rifle qualification badge worn on the right uniform pocket. $1-3

Some GI's used private-purchase hammocks when in the field, preferring them to sleeping in pup tents. The hammock was somewhat cooler. $50-75

After fresh drinking water, fire is arguably the most important requirement for survival. This waterproof plastic case was made to protect wooden matches from the elements.
....$1-3

Radio operator PFC Roy Osborn, C Company, 2nd Battalion, 27th Infantry, 2nd Brigade, 25th Infantry Division, wears a GI towel as a sweatband in this July 1967 photo taken in the Tinh Nghia Province. PFC Osborn has cigarettes, matches and toilet paper tucked into his helmet band – all things that should be kept dry. National Archives photo.

ARMY: Personal Gear

Towels are usually associated with bathing, but in Vietnam these olive-drab towels were primarily used as sweat rags. $10-20

Locally produced and field-made bandanas were also a popular means of combating the heat in Vietnam. This one appears to have been made from a poncho liner. . . $10-20

Sunglasses were popular with troops, and these military-issue Polaroid shades came in a plastic case made by Bachmann Bros. of Philadelphia. . . . . #10-20

The pilot's penlight was issued to Army aviators, but was popular with troops when obtained on the black market.. The lights were marked in small and faint-stamped letters below the pocket clip, "Flashlight, Penlight Type, Pilots" and "U.S."

The aluminum light was powered by two AA batteries. They have a clear lens and a retracting red-shaded lens for night use. Handy and small size, a soldier could hold it in his mouth while map reading and flying in the Huey cockpit at night................. $5-15

Prolonged exposure to the sun was a fact of life in Vietnam. To help prevent uncomfortable burns, the Army provided these 2-ounce tins of Sunburn Preventative Preparation, FSN 8510-162-5658. .... $2-4

Keeping the M16 rifle clean often was literally a matter of life and death. Frequently, troops purchased (or had sent from home) pipe cleaners these to help keep the delicate weapon operating properly. Packets like this were found in the gear of most any GI operating in the field. $1-3

As the designation would suggestion, the M1942 machete was introduced during WWII. The 18-inch steel blade had a two-part plastic grip riveted to it, and was widely used for clearing vegetation on patrol. Originally furnished with a cotton duck sheath, in 1966 this plastic sheath was tried, but found to be less than satisfactory in the tropics................................... $100-150

ARMY: PERSONAL GEAR

One-ounce cans of Desenex Fungicidal Foot Powder were provided to troops in Vietnam. The communal showers used by troops contributed to the spread of foot fungus. Shower shoes and this powder were the only effective means of combating its spread. $3-7

Other memo books available through the Federal Supply Service were bound across the top, providing flip-up access. The size was similar to the left-bound memo books.
. . . . $10-12

Available through the Federal Supply Service were these memo books, which were bound on the left. The green-bound notebooks were sized to fit in the uniform pocket.
. . . . $10-12

Ink pens were stamped "Property U.S. Government," no doubt in an effort to reduce pilferage.
. . . . $8-10

In the field, soldiers often needed to tie things up. Hence, spools of nylon cord, such as this, were desired, if not officially issued, pieces of personal gear
 . . . . $3-7

Virtually every GI carried a sewing kit, which at least contained the materials needed for uniform repair, including needles, thread, buttons and a small pair of scissors. Some were purchased through the PX, others from private vendors in Vietnam, and still others, like this one, homemade back in the States. $15-20

During the Vietnam War, the standard U.S. Army flashlights were the Angle Head Flashlight MX-99/U and the MX-991/U. These were an improvement over the similar-appearing WWII-era TL-122D, the most notable difference being the inclusion of a metal clip on the flashlight base. The light was powered by two "D" cell batteries, and below the battery chamber was a storage compartment holding a spare bulb as well as the spare lens, with a variety of filters.. . . . . **$10-15**

The stainless steel, general-purpose pocketknife was found in the gear of many troops in Vietnam. The knives were made by Imperial, Camillus and others, and are so marked on the blade, along with, in most cases, the date of manufacture. A pin was provided to assist in opening the knife, but this was found to wear holes in the soldier's pockets, so many GIs knocked the pin out. **$35-50**

ARMY: PERSONAL GEAR

This is a civilian private-purchase Cattaraugus 225Q fighting knife. Within the knife-collecting community, there is considerable discussion regarding whether the Cattaraugus 225Q was purchased by the military during WWII, but there is little debate that they were not government-purchase during the Vietnam War. $75-125

Private-purchase Case fighting knife, marked on tang CASE XX and 337-6"Q. Unauthorized weapons created some problems with troops deploying to Vietnam, especially in non-combat units (if there is such a thing) when it came to knives and handguns. It was felt that in untrained hands, ether could produce accidents. Both were viewed with reservation and were sometimes confiscated from unauthorized owners. Fighting knives that have a documented combat history remain desirable as collectibles. $75-125

For centuries, lice have been a plague for soldiers. As had been the case from the closing phases of WWII, in the early stages of American troops operating in Vietnam, DDT-based compounds formed the mainstay of lice control. The familiar 2-ounce tin packaged by McCormick continued to be used, but its color and markings were considerably changed from that of its predecessors, the packaging now being painted olive drab rather than the previously used gray. $5-10

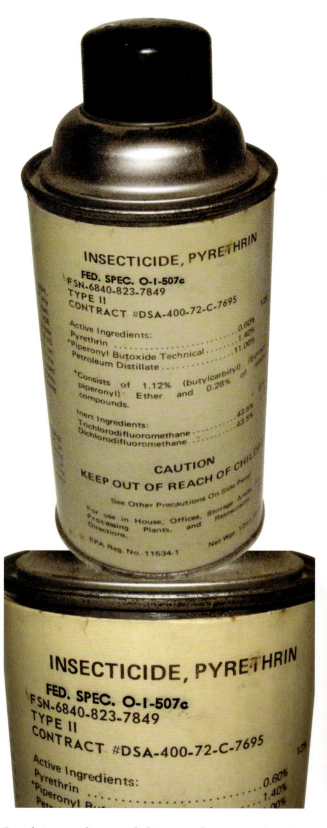

As DDT-resistant strains of lice and mosquitoes were encountered, a new weapon had to be developed. This brought about the development of lindane powder, standardized in 1965. The example shown here was packaged that year by the Octagon Process Co. Lindane was the Army's final attempt to control lice chemically............$3-7

As one would imagine in a tropical environment, insects were a constant nuisance, as well as posing a health risk. The Army issued liquid DEET to be used as a personal mosquito repellent. The "bug juice" was originally issued in 2-ounce white plastic bottles, but because soldiers insisted on carrying them in their helmet bands, the bottle color was changed to olive drab..............$5-10

Pyrethrin was also provided in aerosol cans as an insect repellent, but was not as portable as the 2-ounce bottles of bug juice. $5-10

ARMY: PERSONAL GEAR

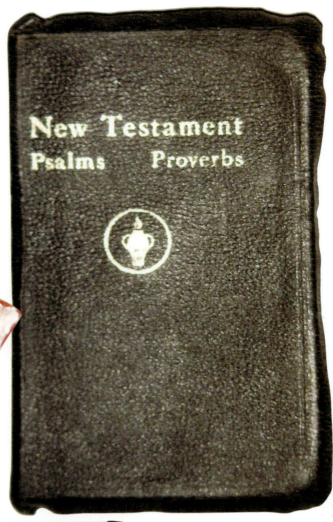

Military regulations require a certain amount of personal hygiene, even in the field. This was the typical type of toothbrush used by troops during the era. **$3-7**

Scripture has provided solace for men in combat for generations, and Vietnam was no different. New Testaments, such as this one, were in the gear of many troops in Southeast Asia. **$5-10**

The footlocker contained the soldier's life while living in the barracks. Everything had a place, and everything was to be in its place. For those who gave their lives in the nation's service, the humble footlocker became the shipping container that returned belongings to their loved one. **$50-100**

211

Military Payment Certificates

In an effort to curb black-market activities, U.S. personnel in Vietnam were not paid in cash, but rather in scrip known is Military Payment Certificates (MPC). During the course of the war, several series were issued, with the series number appearing on the face of each note. The series number is significant, and can be broken down as follows: The first two digits of the series number correspond with the last two digits of the year of printing. The final digit of the series number is a counter for the number of series printed during that year, and is typically 1, for in most cases only one series was used in each year.

When leaving Vietnam, troops could exchange these pay certificates for regular U.S. currency. The series of interest to Vietnam buffs are 591, 611, 641, 651, 661, 681, 691, 692 and 701. It appears that although series 691 was printed, it was not placed into circulation. Beware that reproductions of MPC do exist. (Prices assume "fine" condition.)

Series 611
Five-dollar MPC from 1961. . . . . . **$125**

Photo courtesy of Dennis Mansker.

Photo courtesy of Dennis Mansker.

Series 641
This nickel note is from the first (and only) series of 1965. . . . . $1

Ten-cent notes were also printed. $1

ARMY: MILITARY PAYMENT CERTIFICATES

Photo courtesy of Dennis Mansker.

As were 25-cent denominations.................$2.50

Photo courtesy of Dennis Mansker.

Half-dollar notes were also issued.................$3.50

One-dollar notes were circulated as well.
.... $4

Photo courtesy of Dennis Mansker.

Five-dollar note.
..............$17.50

Photo courtesy of Dennis Mansker.

Photo courtesy of Dennis Mansker.

Ten-dollar note..................................$10

Photo courtesy of Dennis Mansker.

SERIES 661
Nickel. $1.50

Photo courtesy of Dennis Mansker.

Ten cents.....................................$1.50

Warman's Vietnam War Collectibles Identification and Price Guide

Photo courtesy of Dennis Mansker.

Quarter. $2

Photo courtesy of Dennis Mansker.

One dollar. $5

Photo courtesy of Dennis Mansker.

Twenty dollars. $125

SERIES 681
Five-cent note. $2

ARMY: MILITARY PAYMENT CERTIFICATES

This 10-dollar note was illustrated with a Special Forces soldier on the front and a M48 tank on the back.......$30

Twenty dollar. $30

Photos courtesy of Dennis Mansker.

SERIES 692
Twenty-dollar note. $30

Photos courtesy of Dennis Mansker.

Fifty-cent note. $4

NAVY & MARINE CORPS

Marines were involved in some of the most vigorous fighting in Vietnam, much of that at Hue. This is a view of the 2/5 Marines mortar position and command post at Hue University Faculty Apartments. Photo courtesy of USMC History Branch.

U.S. Navy personnel were involved in the Vietnam War for the duration – from the famed "Tonkin Gulf" incident to the evacuation of the U.S. embassy in Saigon. However, little collector interest has developed in Navy memorabilia – perhaps because the centerpieces of such collections are impractical, being either aircraft or ships.

The sister service of the Navy, the U.S. Marines, played a key role in Vietnam, not only in the air, but more notably on the ground. Fierce fighting at Da Nang, Khe Sanh and Hue City proved the mettle of the Marines against the Viet Cong. Marine Corps gear in Vietnam consisted of some new, specially made items, and a considerable amount of gear that was either WWII or Korean War surplus, or hand-me-downs from the Army.

NAVY & MARINE CORPS

This is the Marine Corps blue dress uniform jacket. The Marine dress uniform was, and still is, the most elaborate American military dress uniform. Enlisted men wore a white belt, officers a blue belt.. . . . . $75-125

The trousers worn by all except general officers as part of the blue dress uniform were sky blue. The trousers worn by general officers matched the jacket.
. . . . $50-80

The barracks cover (hat) to be worn with the blue dress uniform was white with black visor. $30-40

WARMAN'S VIETNAM WAR COLLECTIBLES IDENTIFICATION AND PRICE GUIDE

The trousers worn with the service uniform were also green, and of the same cloth as the jacket.
. . . . $20-30

The green, or service uniform, was to be worn while making official visits and calls on American and foreign dignitaries, officials and military officers, and other official, non-combat functions. The jacket was to be worn with the "Service A" configuration, and the shooting badge was to be worn on the left chest.
. . . . $30-40

NAVY & MARINE CORPS

Since the Spanish-American war, the Marine Corps wore khaki during the summer, and during Vietnam War era this was no exception, as the Summer Class A Uniform was khaki. Known to troops as "trops," the jacket is shown here...$20-30

A khaki barracks cover was worn with the Summer Class A Uniform. This is an officer's cover. $30-40

The trousers of the Summer Class A Uniform were also khaki. . $20-30

Khaki Marine Corps web belt.................. $10-15

Marines pin-on Corporal insignia.................. $4-8

Marines pin-on Gunnery Sergeant insignia...... $4-8

The utility uniform was the uniform Marines wore most of the time in Vietnam. Rather than being sewn on, rank insignia are pinned to the jacket collar of the utility uniform. $20-30

The trousers of the utility uniform were made of the same type olive-green cotton as the jacket. $20-30

NAVY & MARINE CORPS

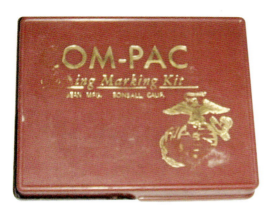

The Com-Pac Clothing Marking Kit was used by individual Marines to stamp their name on their uniform items. It consisted of a handle with letters, numbers and ink..... **$10-20**

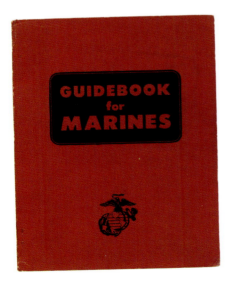

The 11th edition of the "Guidebook for Marines" was published in July 1967 and had a red cover........... **$15-20**

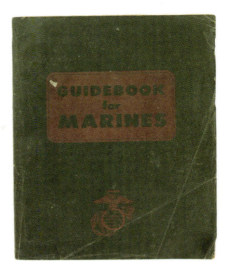

This green-covered "Guidebook for Marines" was the seventh edition of the venerable book and was published in July 1960. Marines everywhere, including those going to Vietnam, were intimately familiar with the contents of this publication. Published by The Leatherneck Association Inc., this thick book was filled with information of all types including close-order drill, personal conduct, operation and cleaning of a wide range of weapons and marksmanship.. **$15-20**

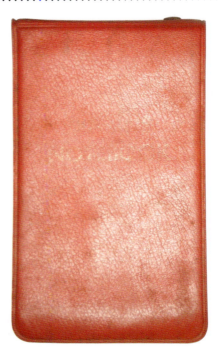

The "red monster" was a small notebook issued to each new recruit. In addition to blank pages, it contained the 11 general orders, Marine traditions and customs, and illustrated lists of all the ranks in all the services, as well as information on weapons...................... **$15-20**

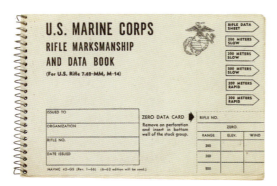

"Every Marine is a rifleman" is an adage of the Corps. This Rifle Marksmanship and Data book was used to track a Marine's scores with the M14 rifle. $5-10

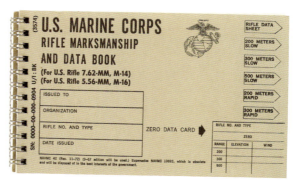

As the M16 began to replace the M14 as the issue rifle for Marines, the Rifle Marksmanship and Data book was revised accordingly. $5-10

U.S. forces in Southeast Asia wore the traditional metal dogtags on chains around their necks. On the tag were the individual's name, serial number and religious affiliation.
. . . .$3-8

This is the Haversack, or upper portion of the USMC M1941 Pack System. It had a blanket-roll strap at the top and a cartridge belt support strap at the bottom. Until recently, the U.S. Marines tended to hold onto older equipment much longer than their Army counter parts. The component shown is the main "haversack" portion of the pack system. Used in conjunction with suspenders and the cartridge belt, these items with contents made up the "Marching Pack" or MP. This canvas pack arrangement was essentially unchanged since WWII and Korea. The WWII-designed Web Gear remained USMC standard issue through 1967 and possibly later. A similar-size bag known as the "knapsack" can be attached below the haversack. A short horse-shoe-shaped blanket roll around the top of the Haversack completed the "Field Marching Pack" or FMP. In Vietnam, about the only time the Marines carried the FMP was from the ship to the dock and then on to their new home at a main support base. After that, like all old campaigners on field operations, the Marines in Vietnam tended to adopt there own web-gear variations to suit their needs and the mission at hand. $30-60

NAVY & MARINE CORPS

The lower portion of the USMC M1941 Pack System was this knapsack. The knapsack was only rarely used in Vietnam. The entire M1941 Pack System consisted of the haversack, knapsack, blanket roll and a pair of suspenders. **$30-60**

The famed Ka-Bar fighting knife has been a part of Marine gear since WWII. The 12-inch knife had a 7-inch blade, and the genuine military Ka-Bar knives have a dull, non-reflective image. **$50-100**

223

U.S. Navy Mark I fighting knife, Mark I with gray Parkerized finish with gray composition and web scabbard. $100-175

Navy gunboat crewman's helmet, based on the helmet developed during WWII for PT boat gun crews. . $50-100

The radio receiver-transmitter RT-159B/URC-4 was tuned to VHF and UHF and came with dual antennas. It was originally intended as a rescue radio, but found use in Vietnam on Patrol Craft Fast. . . . $20-30

NAVY & MARINE CORPS

(Photo courtesy of LaPorte County Historical Society)

M50 ONTOS

Ontos is Greek for "thing" and, given the unusual appearance of this vehicle, with its six recoilless rifles and oddly shaped hull, the name certainly fits.

The Ontos was conceived as a potent, airborne tank destroyer, and in November 1950 the farm machinery division of American industrial giant Allis-Chalmers began work designing this beast. The requirements laid down by the Ordnance office were basic: The engine would be the inline six-cylinder GMC 302 used in the then-new G-749 family of 2-1/2-ton M135/M211 trucks. It was to be coupled to an Allison cross-drive transmission, and its weight and dimension were to permit it to be carried inside the cargo aircraft of the day.

Of the 1,000 units in the original procurement plan, only 297 were produced beginning in 1955. Production ceased in November 1957, and the entire series was rejected by the Army. The Marine Corps was interested, and took delivery of the vehicles. One-hundred-seventy-six of the vehicles were re-powered with a Chrysler 361-cubic-inch V-8 (some sources say 294) beginning in 1963, which required redesigned armored engine covers. The new cover extended forward of the rifle's travel lock, and the engine-access door gained louvers. With the new power plant, the vehicle was redesignated M50A1.

While the six M40A1C 106mm recoilless rifles gave the Ontos tremendous firepower, its shortcoming was the requirement that the vehicle be opened up and a crewman expose himself in order to reload. They began to be phased out of service in the late 1960s.

Weight . . . . 19050 lbs
Size (LxWxH) . . . . 294 x 150.75 x 84
Max Speed . . . . 30 mph
Armament . . . . 6 x 106mm recoilless rifle, 4 x .50 spotting rifle, 1 x .30 caliber machine gun

Too few complete Ontos exist in private hands to establish an accurate value.

LVTP5

The various LVT used during WWII proved the merit of Roebling's amphibious tractor, but also showed room for improvement. Notably, there was a desire to house the troops in a totally enclosed compartment to better protect them during landings. The LVTP5 addressed this concern, and additionally was much larger and had significantly better performance in water, the latter largely the result of the hull front having an inverted-V shape.

Developed in 1951 by the Ingersoll Products Division of Borg-Warner, production began in August 1952. Whereas on previous Amtracs the tracks wrapped around the circumference of the hull, the LVTP5 tracks were mounted low on the hull much like a tank. The inverted grousers on the tracks propelled the vehicle while it was in water. The upper run of track ran an internal return channel to prevent it from providing negative thrust.

The V-shaped bow of the LVTP5 could be lowered to form a ramp for loading and unloading cargo and up to 34 infantry troops (25 for water operation). Additionally, three hatches over the passenger compartment provided alternate means of loading and unloading the vehicle. The crew and passenger compartment was at the front of the vehicle, with the driver's position at the front above the left track channel. The power plant was located at the rear of the vehicle.

Famed Marine sniper Carlos Hathcock was critically burned when a LVTP he was riding in struck a mine in Vietnam.

Weight	87780 lbs
Size (LxWxH)	356 x 140.5 x 103
Max Speed, land	30 mph
Max Speed, water	6.8 mph
Range, land	190 miles

Though obsolete, this vehicle has not become available on the collector market.

NAVY & MARINE CORPS

A M51 of the Third Tank Battalion crosses a river on a landing craft at Dong Ha in June of 1967.

M51

This huge tank retriever was created using the suspension and automotive components of the M103 heavy tank. Just as the M103 was shunned by the Army but used by the Marines, so it was with the M51. The U.S. Marine Corps adopted the M51 in 1958 and used it through the Vietnam War and beyond. The Army preferred the M88.

Four men operated the M51, which was equipped with a hydraulically driven 45-ton-capacity recovery winch as well as a 5-ton auxiliary winch. A large, hydraulically actuated boom was mounted toward the rear of the vehicle. Anchor blades, also raised and lowered hydraulically, were provided on both the front and rear to stabilize the M51 during recovery and lifting operations.

Weight . . . . 120000 lbs
Size (LxWxH) . . . . 399 x 143 x 129
Max Speed . . . . 30 mph
Range . . . . 200 miles

Not readily available.

AIR FORCE

U.S. Air Force personnel were flying combat missions in Vietnam as early as 1961, although some sources indicate crews were assisting Free French forces fighting in Vietnam as far back as 1954. Despite being among the first in and last out of the country, and several notable POWs being Air Force personnel, Vietnam-era U.S.A.F. gear has attracted little collector interest compared to Army equipment. What follows is a representative sampling of items in this niche of collecting.

AIR FORCE

Tactical Air Command patch
..........................$10-20

Pacific Air Forces patch $10-20

Military Airlift Command patch
..........................$5-10

First Special Operations Wing patch
..........................$50-100

555th Tactical Fighter Squadron patch
..........................$20-30

F-101 patch $25-50

B-57 patch
.....$50-75

AC-130A patch $25-50

Stinger – Vengeance by Night, 18th Special Operations Squadron patch, AC-1119K crew $25-50

Peace Hell Bomb Hanoi patch
. . . . $10-20

Advise and Assist patch $15-20

Flight helmet with oxygen mask: A common U.S. Air Force flying helmet used with oxygen-equipped aircraft during the Vietnam War was the single-visor HGU-2A/P, which was based on the HGU-22/P helmet shell. $100-150

Flight helmet: Aircraft crewmen who required communications equipment without oxygen service, such as spotter and helicopter crewmen, used the HGU-27
. . . . $75-125

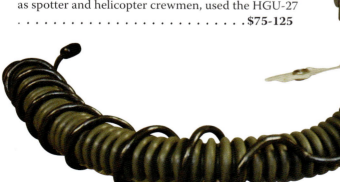

AIR FORCE

H-79/A1C headset: This electrical headset and microphone included connecting cords, plugs, jacks and switches. It was worn by flight personnel, and could be used with certain helmets, or with soft head covers. The NSN is 5965-00-839-8990. . . . . **$20-30**

Garrison Cap: This Air Force officer's blue garrison cap displays the rank of full colonel. **$20-30**

Field Grade Officer's Service Cap: The "lightning bolts" on the visor indicate this is the cap of a male officer with rank of Lt. Col. or higher. **$50-75**

Warman's Vietnam War Collectibles Identification and Price Guide

Formal Black Service Cap: Worn with U.S. Air Force formal dress uniform. $40-60

Officer's Service Cap: This blue service cap was Air Force standard. $40-60

Woman's Air Force Service Hat: This blue and white hat was worn with the Class "A" uniform. $10-15

AIR FORCE

Fatigue uniform jacket: Typical of the cross-service standardization prevalent since Defense Secretary Robert McNamara's time, U.S. Air Force personnel in Vietnam wore uniforms like their army counterparts. Early Vietnam-era Air Force uniforms, such as this first-pattern piece, had blue name and branch tapes on them. $30-60

Fatigue uniform jacket: Later uniforms, like this third-pattern jacket, replaced the blue tapes with more subdued OD and black identifiers. $30-60

(Photo courtesy of http://grunts.free.fr)

Fatigue uniform jacket: Vietnam fourth-model jungle jacket ripstop U.S. Air Force with in-country rank chevrons and tapes. . . . $50-100

K-2B Flight Suit: This was the standard U.S. Air Force flight suit during Vietnam. $50-100

K-2B Flight Suit, modified: Some personnel modified their suits, shortening the sleeves, in response to the hot conditions found in Vietnam. $50-100

MA-1 Flight Jacket: Officially known as "Jacket, Flyers, Man's Intermediate Type MA-1," this lightweight nylon jacket was introduced in the mid-1950s and remained in use through the mid-1980s. $100-200

AIR FORCE

Party Suit: These were a local and unofficial creation that arose in 1967. Known as "special flight suits," the 8th Tactical Fighter Wing used these black-dyed cotton flight suits for social occasions. The colorful, lightweight suits, popularly called "party suits," were soon adopted by the Air Force flying units stationed at the large bases in Thailand. The tradition also quickly spread to units in South Vietnam. Party suits were normally limited to flight personnel and those in direct support of flight operations. **$250-350**

SRU-21/P vest: The Air Force used this survival vest for all aircrews beginning in 1967-68. Army aviators, and occasionally Special Forces, used them as well. **$175-200**

(Photo courtesy of http://grunts.free.fr)

AIR FORCE

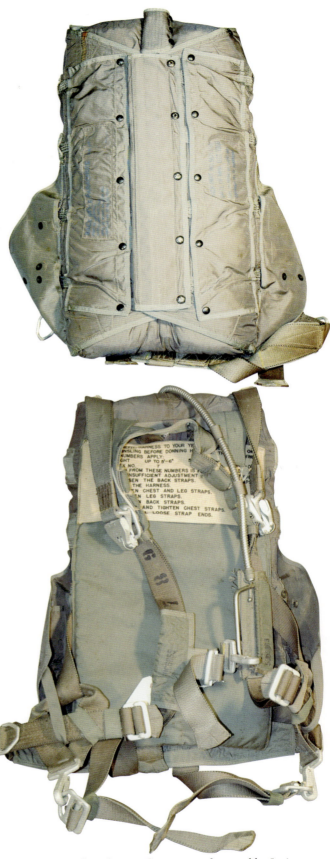

SRU-19/P survival chaps: Originally intended for SAC bomber crews, these lightweight survival chaps were intended to be a means for aircrew to carry variety of survival gear. However, the vest was found to be more comfortable, and by 1967 the chaps were being phased out **$175-200**

Parachute: Back-style parachute, manufactured by Irving Air Chute Co., with harness and pack assembly.. **$150-250**

Distress marker light: SDU-5/E strobe light used by pilots and elite units. The lamp, FSN 6230-067-5209, is furnished with a lanyard, because it will sink. $50-60

ACR RT-10 Receiver-Transmitter, Radio: Pilot's emergency radio, air/sea rescue, in metal case. Extending the antenna turns the radio on. $40-60

RT 159B/URC Radio Receiver-Transmitter: Pilot's portable emergency transceiver with extendable "rabbit ears" antenna. This radio was reportedly also used by Navy swift boat crewmen. $40-60

AIR FORCE

Pilot's Survival Knife: Made by Camillus Cutlery Co., this knife came in a sheath with a carborundum stone. The knife's pommel was designed so it could be used as a hammer... $30-60

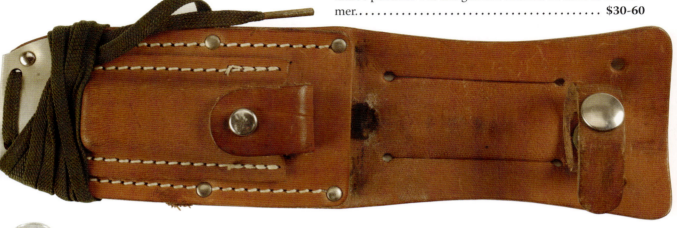

MC-1 Parachute Survival knife: This knife has two blades, a hook and a snap. The hook blade was designed for quick cutting of parachute suspension lines. The snap blade was for general use. $60-100

(Photo courtesy of http://grunts.free.fr)

Mk-3 Signaling Mirror: This 3" x 5" mirror was made for use by downed pilots to signal ships or aircraft for rescue. Comes in a protective sleeve. $15-25

(Photo courtesy of http://grunts.free.fr)

WAR TROPHIES

(Photo courtesy of Don F. Pratt Museum)

(Photo courtesy of U.S. Army Transportation Museum)

For centuries, whenever men have gone off to war, they returned with souvenirs of their travels, and sometimes their conquests. For many soldiers returning from Vietnam, the only souvenirs they brought back were their lives, their memories and photographs. Oftentimes the photos captured exotic sites of a land far away from their homes, and the laughing faces of their buddies and comrades at arms.

These personal photos are near priceless to veterans and loved ones – but sadly mean little to others, and to future generations. If you are a veteran, or have a veteran in your family, get out those photos and slides and write down who the people are staring back at you and jot down the location where it was snapped. These simple steps will help preserve the legacy, and your family history, for future generations.

Other soldiers brought back currency, flags, jackets or bits of enemy gear, sometimes known as a "battlefield pick up." Some soldiers bartered for gear from our ARVN or Australian allies as souvenirs.

WAR TROPHIES

(Photo courtesy of U.S. Army Transportation Museum)

This is a NVA hand-grenade carrier, intended to carry two ChiCom Pull Friction Fuse long-handle grenades used by the VC and NVA. The metallic head is carried head down in the pouches at the bottom. The 8-inch wood handles are secured with the small tie tapes. A similar model with provision to carry four grenades was also used. . . . . . . **No established value**

(Photo courtesy of U.S. Army Transportation Museum)

241

This is a Chinese Communist copy of the U.S. WWII "pocket-watch style" magnetic compass provided to the North Vietnamese Army, with Chinese characters on the compass face. Even though the brass compass case is dented and well worn, it has the original-issue box and 10-page instruction booklet dated 1963. . . . . **No established value**

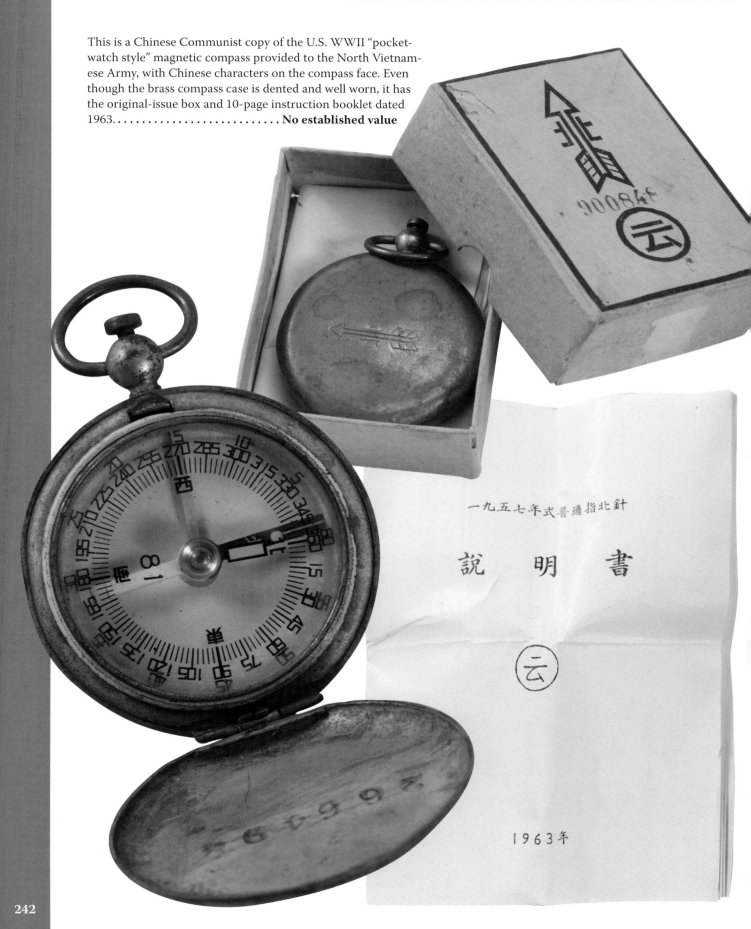

WAR TROPHIES

This is a three-pocket NVA rucksack. NVA items tended to be of very simple construction.
.... $20-40

An example of a two-pocket VC/NVA rucksack.... $85-150

The ARVN two-pocket rucksack differed from both the U.S. and the NVA rucksack. $20-40

WARMAN'S VIETNAM WAR COLLECTIBLES IDENTIFICATION AND PRICE GUIDE

The Viet Cong typically used Chinese stick grenades that were themselves copies of WWII Japanese designs. The most common of these was the fragmentation grenade. Obviously, it would be unwise to display a live grenade, and the stability of such items is questionable. Hence, most of those in collections are reproductions or were professionally rendered inert at the time of capture. $30-40

North Vietnamese pith helmet with camo cover, and material salvaged from camo parachute cloth inserted in netting. $30-50

WAR TROPHIES

Very rare, North Vietnamese camouflage holder. Roughly 8 inches in diameter, these handmade items are constructed of metal rings and a bamboo frame. These were worn by enemy soldiers on the back or on top of the rucksack when on the North Vietnamese.

The Viet Cong were masters at camouflage discipline. Fresh local vegetation is inserted into the ring to offer concealment from overhead aircraft. As the terrain and vegetation changed, each soldier removed the old and inserted new vegetation in the camouflage of the man in front on him. Green camouflage parachute cloth salvaged from supply drops was also used as a cape tied over the enemy soldier's shoulders. $75-150

The carrier used by NVA for the canteen was a simple affair made of webbing. The canteen was made in China and held about one quart.
.... $20-35

The NVA, not surprisingly, were supplied with entrenching tools made in China. They had wooden handles and a steel blade. $25-40

The NVA used rocket-propelled grenades effectively against U.S. armor in Vietnam. The weapon of choice was the locally made copy of the Soviet RPG2, known as the B40 or B50. Inert examples of these rounds are popular trophies and display items.
.... $40-60

WAR TROPHIES

The PPSh41 submachine gun was developed in Russia during WWII. Firing up to 900 rounds of 7.62mm ammunition per minute, the weapon found widespread use with other nations' armies, including the North Vietnamese, who dubbed it the K-50. Ownership of a fully automatic example in the United States is strictly regulated.

Dummy $175-350
Semi-automatic $900-1100
Fully automatic $13,000-15,000

The NVA snipers were typically armed with the excellent Mosin-Nagant 91/30PU rifle. Firing a 7.62x54r round, the rifle had an effective range of several hundred yards............................. $400-1,200

The AK-47 is arguably the most widely recognized, and widely used, automatic weapon in the world. Mikhail Kalashnikov designed the weapon in the Soviet Union in 1947, and it has been exported and produced worldwide since. The NVA used Soviet, Chinese and locally made examples of the AK-47. Ownership of a fully automatic example in the United States is strictly regulated.

Dummy $175-350
Semi-automatic $900-1100
Fully automatic $13,000-15,000

Bayonets were produced for use with the SKS as well...... $40-60

The local tailoring industry flourished while U.S. troops were in Vietnam and many of these businesses catered to military personnel. This souvenir jacket appears to have been crafted from a poncho liner with extensive embroidery. Prices on such items vary widely depending on craftsmanship, provenance and decoration..... $100-500

WAR TROPHIES

VIETNAMESE CURRENCY

Photo courtesy of Dennis Mansker

Although universally referred to as "piasters," Vietnamese currency was actually denominated in dong. This is a 20-dong note. .... $.25-.75

Photo courtesy of Dennis Mansker

A 50-dong note.. .... $1

Photo courtesy of Dennis Mansker

This is a 100-dong note; the area that appears blank actually contains a water mark. .... $.25-1

Photo courtesy of Dennis Mansker

The 1,000-dong note. .... $.50

This was the flag of the Republic of Vietnam until its April 30, 1975, surrender. It had been designed by Emperor Thành Thái in 1880, and consisted of a yellow field with three horizontal red stripes running through it.. $40-100

One of the most popular war trophies was the flag of the National Liberation Front, or Viet Cong. The red and blue banner had a Communist star centered on it............ $40-100

INDEX

101st Airborne Division, 24, 112, 202
11th Armored Cavalry, 19, 202
11th Light Infantry Brigade, 201
12th Signal Group, 151
15th Artillery, 75
173rd Airborne Brigade, 201
18th Brigade, 24
18th Engineer Brigade, 202
18th Military Police Brigade, 202
198th Light Infantry Brigade, 202
199th Light Infantry Brigade, 95, 202
1st ARVN Division, 26
1st ARVN Engineer Battalion, 26
1st Aviation Brigade, 201
1st Battalion, 106, 130
1st Cavalry Division, 31, 106, 201
1st Cavalry Division (Airmobile), 106
1st Infantry Division, 202
1st Logistical Command, 183, 201
1st Signal Brigade, 142-143, 151
1st Squadron, 31
20th Engineer Brigade, 201
25th Infantry Division, 82, 101, 119, 135, 146, 200, 204
27th Battalion, 24
27th Infantry, 82, 119, 135, 204
2nd Battalion, 82, 95, 119, 135, 140, 190, 204
2nd Brigade, 204
2nd Platoon, 146
2nd Signal Group, 144
327th Signal Company, 144
34th Armor, 190
362nd Signal Company, 144
3rd Infantry, 95
3rd Squadron, 19
41st Signal Battalion, 151
44th Medical Brigade, 201
45th Engineer Group, 24, 26
4th Cavalry, 19
4th Infantry Division, 178, 200
502nd Infantry, 140
510th Signal Company, 143
525-3-1 Military Operations Lessons Learned Military Engineering, 188
530B Pumper, 175
555th Tactical Fighter Squadron, 229
5th Artillery Group, 130
5th Infantry, 106, 201
5th Special Force Group, 202
73rd Signal Battalion, 143
75th Infantry Regiment, 68
7th Battalion, 75
82nd Airborne Division, 202
83rd Artillery, 130
8th Tactical Fighter Wing, 235
984th Land Clearing Company, 22
9th Cavalry, 31
9th Infantry Division, 200
Abrams, General Creighton, 80
AC-130A, 230
ACF-Brill, 163
ACP ammo, 46
Advise and Assist, 230
Aerial Cutlery, 51
Aggressor, 127
Air Force, 3, 5, 34, 180-181, 228, 230-236
Air Medal, 198
AK-47, 247
Allis-Chalmers, 225
Allison Division, 54, 66
altar, 12-13
AM 350-12 Guide for Squad Leaders, 196
AM General, 157
ambulance, 8, 156, 158, 162, 166
Americal Division (23rd Infantry Division), 201
American Motors Corp., 159
ammunition, 3, 29, 32-33, 36-37, 44-45, 54, 60, 88, 98, 106-107, 110, 183, 188, 247
An Khe, 27, 116
An Lao Valley, 31
antenna, 145-147, 149-150, 238
Antifogging Kit, 18
Armed Forces Expeditionary Medal, 200
Armed Services Electro Standards Agency, 164
armor, body, 93-94
Armored Cavalry Vehicle, 57
Armored Command and Reconnaissance Carrier, 58
armored personnel carrier, 21, 56, 58
Army Commendation Medal, 199
Army Digest, 182
Army Materiel Command, 71
Army Medical Service, 8
arsenal, 5, 32-33, 37
artillery, 3, 21, 28-30, 46, 60, 66, 75, 112, 130, 193
ARVN, 26, 33, 37, 45, 53, 57, 81, 240, 243
Australia, 185
Aviation, 5, 79, 169, 201
B-57, 229
bag, 9, 17, 25, 45, 49, 73, 86-87, 91, 102, 104-105, 107-108, 114-116, 134-136, 146, 149, 151-152, 222
bandage, 9
bandana, 9
bandoleer, 44-45, 106
Barnabas, Chaplain (Maj) Daniel, 15
barracks cover, 217, 219
Bata, 70
Battery C, 130
Battle of Ap Bac, 57
Bauer Ordnance Co., 52
bayonet, 50-52
Be Your Own Inspector, 186
belt, 10, 45, 83-84, 88-89, 107, 111, 122, 126, 151-152, 217, 220, 222
Beo-Gam, 124, 128
beret, 81
bipod, 21, 38, 43, 192
blanket, 87, 222-223
blasting cap, 24-25, 49
Blasting Machine, 24-25
Blaw-Knox Co., 59
Boobytraps, 189
boot, 68-72
Borg-Warner, 226
Bowen-McLaughlin-York, 64-67
Bronze Star, 198
Browning, 31, 38
brush, 40-41, 173
Buffalo Arms Co., 37
bulldozer, 26, 67
C Company, 204
C Troop, 19
C-130, 27
C-4, 24-25
Cadillac, 53, 63, 66, 180
Cambodia, 10, 12, 19, 99, 106
Camillus, 152, 208, 239
camouflage, 76-77, 80-81, 119, 123-124, 126-128, 169-170, 245
Cam Rahn Bay, 14
canteen, 85-86, 109, 116, 246
Can Tho Army Airfield, 11
cap, 24-25, 49, 78-79, 85, 149, 231-232
case (or Case), 10, 14-15, 25, 42-43, 46-48, 88, 100, 103, 105, 107, 111-112, 115, 117, 131-132, 134-135, 137, 145, 149-150, 157, 159, 162, 169-170, 175-177, 179, 204-205, 209-210, 238, 242

Caterpillar, 178
Cattaraugus, 209
Central Highlands, 75, 120
chaplain, 3, 5, 12-15
chaps, 237
charge assembly, 25
Chemical Corps, 3, 5, 17
Chien Cu: War Material Used by the Viet Cong ..., 186
Chieu Hoi, 98
Chinese Communist, 242
Chrysler, 56, 58, 66, 180, 225
cigarettes, 75, 131, 133-134, 204
Claymore, 44, 49, 102
cleaning kit, 32, 40, 42
coat, 27, 121-123
Cold War, 39, 127
Collins, Harold, 146
Colt, 34, 36, 43, 52
Columbus Milpar & Mfg., 51
Company A, 106, 140
Company C, 26, 146
Company D, 95
Company H (Ranger), 68
compass, 10, 111-113, 193, 242
Consolidated Diesel Electric Co., 177
Corporal, 220
Corps of Engineers, 22-27
Counter Insurgency Support Office, 124, 128
crypto set, 148
Da Nang, 216
DA Pam 381-10 Weapons and Equipment Recognition Guide Southeast Asia, 188
DA Pam 381-12 Recognition Guide of Ammunition ..., 188
DA Pam 550-55 Area Handbook for South Vietnam, 189
Dak To, 115
Dalat, 143
DEET, 210
demolition, 24-25, 189
Department of the Army Pamphlet 750-1, 196
Desert Storm, 54
desk, 96
destructive device, 28, 36, 39
detonation cord, 24-25
Distinguished Flying Cross, 199
Distinguished Service Cross, 197-198
Distinguished Service Medal, 198
Distress marker light, 238
Dodge, 162-163, 165-166

dogtags, 222
dong, 68, 227, 249
Dong Ha, 227
Dong Nai River, 68
dress uniform, 217, 232
duffel bag, 73, 116
DUKW, 179
Duster, 61, 115
Eifler, Major General Charles W., 79
Emperor Thành Thái, 250
Engineer Research and Development Laboratory, 123
entrenching tool, 91, 117-118
Explosive Ordnance Disposal Team, 24
F-101, 229
fatigue, 121-122, 233
Federal Stock Number, 7, 94, 164
field pack, 88-89, 112, 186
Fire Base Exodus, 15, 20
Fire Support Base Saint Barbara, 190
firefighting, 27
First Logistical Command, 79
First Special Operations Wing, 229
first-aid kit, 8
flag, 13-14, 250
flare, 104
flashlight, 153, 206, 208
Flight helmet, 230
flight suit, 234
flyer, 78
FM 21-13, The Soldiers Guide, 189
FM 21-15, Care and Use of Individual Clothing and Equipment, 189
FM 21-26 Map Reading, 190
FM 21-41 Soldier's Handbook for Chemical and Biological ..., 190
FM 24-20 Field Wire and Field Cable Techniques, 191
FM 31-15 Operations Against Irregular Forces, 191
FM 5-34 Engineer Field Data, 189
Food Machinery Corp., 56-58, 64-65
foot powder, 203, 207
footlocker, 211
Ford Motor Co., 156
Fort Lewis, Wash., 144
Fort Monmouth, N.J., 164
Free French, 228
fuel, 7, 53, 55, 61, 136-137, 156-157, 168-170, 177, 183, 186
fuse, 19, 25, 241
Garand, 32, 45-46, 50, 98
gas mask, 17, 186
General Motors, 34, 37, 54, 57, 66

Geneva Convention, 162
GOER, 178
Good Conduct Medal, 198
Graphical Training Aid, 98
Green Berets, 128
grenade, 19, 28, 35-36, 48, 57, 68, 92-94, 244
Guide Lamp Division, 34
gunboat, 224
Gunnery Sergeant, 220
hammock, 101, 203
Handy Talkie, 144
hat, 78-81, 217, 232
Hathcock, Carlos, 226
haversack, 25, 222-223
headset, 78, 150, 231
Heavy Hints for Light Packs, 186
helicopter, 8, 20, 72, 78, 141, 230
helmet, 75-78, 94, 204, 210, 224, 230, 244
Hi-Lite, 184
howitzer, 30, 62, 65-66
Hue, 26, 216
Hue University Faculty Apartments, 216
Husky, 59
I Field Force Vietnam, 200
Imperial Knife, 51
Ingersoll Products Division, 226
insignia, 3, 13, 143, 185, 197, 200, 220
International Latex Corp., 85
Irving Air Chute Co., 237
Ithaca, 34
jacket, 93-94, 121-124, 217-220, 233-234, 248
Jay Bee Corp., 112
Joint Services Commendation Medal, 199
Ka-Bar, 223
Kaiser M715, 165
Kaiser M725 ambulance, 166
Kaiser-Jeep Corporation, 157
Kalashnikov, Mikhail, 247
Keep Clean Fuel Clean, 186
khaki, 108, 219-220
Khe Sanh, 24, 216
knapsack, 222-223
knife, 51-52, 138-140, 151-152, 203, 208-209, 223-224, 239
knives, 3, 28, 50, 152, 208-209, 223
Krug, Ronald, 35
Lance missile carrier, 60
Landing Zone Bronco, 10, 99
Landing Zone Hammond, 148

INDEX

Lang Bien Mountain, 143
LARC-V, 179
launcher, 35-36, 39, 54, 57, 68, 92
laundry bag, 108
Leatherneck Association Inc., 221
Leatherwood, 32
Legion of Merit, 199
Leopard Spot Pattern, 124
LeTourneau-Westinghouse, 179
lice, 210
Light Antitank Weapon, 39
Lindane, 210
lineman, 151-152
litter, 156
Long Binh, 95
lubricant, 96
LVTP5, 226
M109 Van Trucks, 171
M123A1C Truck Tractor, 177
M151, 14, 148, 155-157
M170 Battlefield Ambulance, 156
M274 Mule, 161
M275 Tractor Trucks, 172
M292A1 Expansible Van, 173
M328 Bridge Trucks, 177
M342A2 Dump Truck, 174
M35A2 Cargo Truck, 168
M38, 155-156
M422 Mighty-Mite, 159
M422A1 Mighty-Mite, 160
M49A2C Fuel Tanker Truck, 169
M50 Ontos, 225
M50A1 Water Tanker Truck, 170
M51, 227
M51A2 Dump Truck with Winch, 176
M52A2 Tractor Truck, 176
M54A2 Five-Ton Cargo Truck, 175
M60, 29, 37-38, 45, 55, 57, 67, 96, 193
M718, 158
M726 Telephone Maintenance Truck, 167
M756A2 Pipeline Construction Truck, 174
machete, 91, 206
machine gun, 29, 37-38, 45, 56-58, 61, 66, 193, 225
Mack, 175-177
magazines, 43, 110
manual, 105, 162, 168, 182, 188-195
map, 112-113, 117, 190, 193, 206
Marching Pack, 222
Marines, 3, 34, 66, 145, 155, 159, 161, 216, 220-222, 227
marksmanship, 42, 188, 191, 221-222

Martin, Harold, 151
McCormick, 210
McNamara, Robert, 233
Medal of Honor, 12, 197
Mekong Delta, 74, 82
Meritorious Unit Commendation, 144
Mermite, 140-141
mess kit, 137-140
Mid-America Research Corp, 159
Military Airlift Command, 229
Military Assistance Command, Vietnam, 200
Military Payment Certificates, 212
mine, 23, 44, 49, 102, 226
ministers, 12
mortar, 12, 21, 58, 216
Mosin-Nagant, 247
MUTT, 156-157
Natick Laboratories, 71
National Defense Service Medal, 199
National Firearms Act, 36
National Liberation Front, 250
NATO, 45, 168
notebook, 221
NVA, 186, 241, 243, 246-247
Octagon Process Co., 210
Okinawa, 124
Ontario Knife Co., 52
opener, 134, 136
Operation and Preventive Maintenance M16A1 Rifle, 192
Operator's Manual for the M60 Machine Gun, 193
ordnance, 3, 17, 24, 28, 48, 52, 174-175, 225
Ordnance Corps, 3, 17, 28, 174
Ordnance Tank Automotive Command, 175
organ, 16
Osborn, Roy, 204
overshoes, 73
oxygen mask, 230
Pacific Air Forces, 229
Pacific Car and Foundry Co., 59
Paffel, Steven, 68
Paige sighting device, 42
PAM 350-13 Guide for Platoon Sergeants, 196
parachute, 237, 239, 244-245
parachutist, 48
Party Suit, 235
pasters, 40
patient slippers, 72
Patton, 55

Peace Hell Bomb Hanoi, 230
penlight, 203, 206
periscope, 56
Pershing, 55
photography, 5, 142
piasters, 249
pipe cleaners, 206
pistol, 31, 33, 88
pith helmet, 244
Plei Dejerang, 142
Pocket Guide to Vietnam, 184-185
Polaroid, 205
pole, 100, 152
poncho, 84, 205, 248
pouch, 10, 105, 109-112, 151
POWs, 228
PS Magazine, 187, 192-193
Punji sticks, 71, 74
Purple Heart, 198
PX, 79, 207
Pyrethrin, 210
Quartermaster Corps, 3, 68-69, 91, 130, 134-135
R-2 Crash Truck, 163
radio, 2, 20, 53, 58-59, 63, 95, 142-149, 153, 156, 195, 204, 224, 238
Ranger, 68, 81
rations, 3, 69, 130-136
RB 61-1 Vol 1, Reference Book, The Division, 188
reeling machine, 152
Ridgeway, Matthew Bunker, 78
rifle, 29, 32, 34, 36, 42-43, 45, 48, 66, 81, 97-98, 110, 192, 203, 206, 222, 225, 247
rifle bore cleaner, 97
Rock Island Arsenal, 32, 37
rocket, 39
Rome Plows, 22
ROTCM 145-30 Individual Weapons and Marksmanship, 188
Rubber Duckies, 37
rucksack, 86, 91-92, 107, 243, 245
SAC bomber, 237
Saginaw Steering Gear Div., 37
Saigon, 7, 35, 184, 216
sandals, 73
sandbag, 99
Savasky, Stephen, 142
scabbard, 50-51, 224
Scorpion, 63
Scripture, 211
service uniform, 218
sewing kit, 207

sharpshooter, 203
Sheridan, 54, 101
shirt, 93, 120, 122, 124
shoe, 74
shotgun, 36, 107
shower pail, 102
Signal Corps, 3, 5, 60, 115, 142, 146, 151-152, 164, 191
Signaling Mirror, 239
Silver Star, 198
Simmonds, 43
sleeping bag, 91, 114-115
sling, 46, 90
Smith and Wesson, 31
sniper, 22, 29, 32, 46, 48, 226
soap, 103
socks, 74, 120
Soldier's Medal, 199
Soviet, 39, 54, 246-247
Special Forces, 81, 85, 124, 127-128, 215, 236
spike, 71
stake, 177
State Department Publication No. 7724, 185
Stillwell, General Joseph "Vinegar Joe", 175
Stinger – Vengeance by Night, 18th Special Operations Squadron, 230
Stocker and Yale, 112
Stoner, Eugene, 34
stove, 137, 182
Strategic Communications Command, 143
stripper clips, 44
Subsistence Research Laboratory, 134
sunburn, 206

sunglasses, 205
Superior Magneto, 112
Supply Catalog, 191
survival kit, 103-104
suspenders, 88, 91, 111-112, 222-223
switchboard, 153
Tactical Air Command, 229
Tactical Information Command Van, 142
tank, 53-55, 61-63, 66-67, 81, 101, 130, 169-170, 175, 193, 215, 225-227
tape recorder, 16
target, 42, 54, 98, 145-146, 203
tear gas, 17, 190
telephone, 5, 142, 150-153, 164, 167, 173, 195
telescope, 47
tent, 100
Thailand, 144, 185, 235
The 8 Week Challenge – Your New World, 185
Third Tank Battalion, 227
Thompson, 33-34
tiger stripe, 119
Tinh Nghia Province, 146, 204
TM 10-276 Hot Weather Clothing and Equipment, 194
TM 10-405 Army Mess Operations, 194
TM 10-412-5 Army Recipes …, 194
TM 21-305, Motor Vehicles Manual for the Wheeled Vehicle Driver, 195
TM 55-310 Truckmaster's Handbook, 195
TM 9-1005-223-10 Operator's Manual for Rifle …, 192
TM 9-1290-333-15 Operator's, Organizational, Direct Support …, 193

TNT, 24-25
Tonkin Gulf, 216
toothbrush, 211
Torah, 14
towel, 204
Transportation Corps, 3, 154
trench art, 75
tripod, 38, 46
Troop B, 31
trousers, 123, 126-129, 217-220
tunnel rats, 17, 103, 190
U.S. Army Engineer Command, Vietnam, 202
underwear, 120
uniform, 13, 119, 124, 127, 189, 203, 207, 217-221, 232-233
Uniforms of Seven Allies, 185
United States Armor Board, 178
United States Army, Vietnam, 200
Uptight US Army in Vietnam, 184
V-100/M706 Commando, 180
V-41/GT Signal Corps Telephone Maintenance Truck, 164
Velcro, 94
vest, 92, 94, 236-237
Viet Cong, 17, 20, 33, 74, 98, 186, 188, 216, 244-245, 250
Vietnam Campaign Medal, 197
Vietnam Service Medal, 197
Vietnamese Currency, 249
Walker Bulldog, 53
John Wayne, 128, 134
Weapons Oil Medium, 97
Westmoreland, General William, 145
Willys-Overland Motors, 155
Witness Statement on Individual, 105
XM177E1, 36
XM177E2, 36
XM706E2 Commando, 181

More Military Memorabilia References

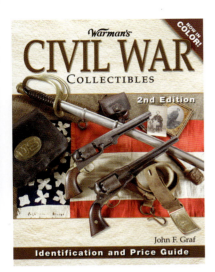

Warman's® Civil War Collectibles
Identification and Price Guide
2nd Edition
by John F. Graf
This spectacular guide to Civil War memorabilia features 3,500 listings including firearms, currency, uniforms and more.
Softcover • 8-1/4 x 10-7/8 • 416 pages
1,000 color photos
Item# WCVWC2 • $29.99

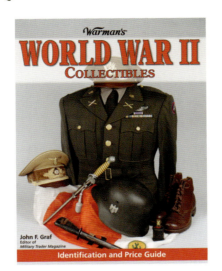

Warman's® World War II Collectibles
Identification and Price Guide
by John F. Graf
Get pricing and historical details about World War II collectibles such as helmets, uniforms, firearms, daggers and mementos, in this extensive full-color book.
Softcover • 8-1/4 x 10-7/8 • 256 pages
1,000 color photos
Item# Z0972 • $24.99

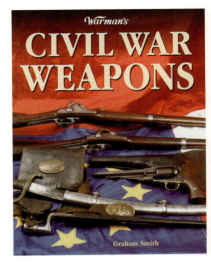

Warman's® Civil War Weapons
by Graham Smith
Review more than 400 stunning color photos of 100+ weapons and military vehicles used by Confederate and Union Army soldiers. Explore handguns, shoulder arms, and ground vehicles, among other items.
Softcover • 8-¼ x 10-7/8 • 256 pages
400+ color photos
Item# WCWW • $24.99

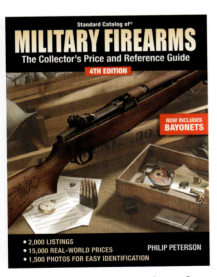

Standard Catalog of® Military Firearms
The Collector's Price and Reference Guide
4th Edition
by Phillip Peterson
This ground-breaking fourth edition of the all-inclusive military firearms guide includes, for the first time, bayonets! Explore more than 300 years of military firearms from around the world, with real-world values and background information.
Softcover • 8-1/4 x 10-7/8 • 520 pages
1,400
Item# Z0741 • $29.99

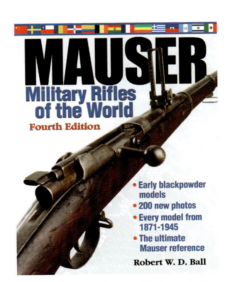

Mauser Military Rifles of the World
4th Edition
by Robert W.D. Ball
Get more Mauser, more of the time with this full-color guide. Featuring many never-before published photos, this book covers rifles from 50 countries, with historical data about military conflicts involving Mauser.
Hardcover • 8-1/4 x 10-7/8 • 448 pages
1,300+ color photos
Item# Z0322 • $49.99

To Order

Call the publisher at
800-258-0929
M-F 8 am – 5 pm

Visit online at
www.krausebooks.com

OR

Go to booksellers nationwide and select antiques shops nationwide to pick up a copy!

Please mention offer code **ACB8** with all direct-to-publisher orders.

SUBSCRIBE TODAY TO MILITARY TRADER
Get 1 year (12 BIG ISSUES) for just $19.98! AND SAVE 66%!

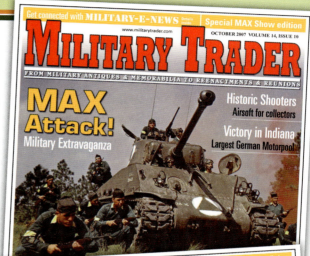

Find all of the military collectibles you'll ever need, including uniforms, helmets, field gear, weapons and more, inside each issue of *Military Trader!*

Here's a look at what you'll find each month:

- Monthly features on presentation and restoration of your collectibles
- Valuable collecting hints
- An up-to-date show directory
- Price trends so you can discover the best values and make the best deals
- and much, much more!

DON'T WAIT!
Log on to
www.militarytrader.com
and subscribe today.

Get 1 year (12 BIG ISSUES) **for just $19.98!**

Or call 866-700-2994. Outside the U.S. and Canada, call 386-246-3425. You can also write us at: P.O. Box 420235, Palm Coast, FL 32142-0235. Mention offer code J8AHAD.

In Canada: add $15 (includes GST/HST). Outside the U.S. and Canada: add $23. Outside the U.S., remit payment in U.S. funds with order. Please allow 4-6 weeks for first-issue delivery. Annual newsstand rate $59.88.

SAVE 66%